TRIBAL DEVELOPMENT PLANS

About the Author

S.G. Deogaonkar is a scholar of repute and his field of specialisation is Political and Social Anthropology, Tribal Development and Constitutional Law. He has participated in numerous conferences and seminars including the Xth International Congress of Anthropological and Ethnological Sciences. He was a Member on the District Planning and Development Council of the Chandrapur District and Chancellor's Nominee on the Nagpur University Senate. Dr. Deogaonkar was a Member-participant of the Socio-Economic Groups on scheduled Castes and Scheduled Tribes for formulation of the Eighth Five Year Plan Schemes constituted under the Backward Classes Division of the Planning Commission. He has completed many post- doctoral research projects for the UGC and ICSSR and was a National (Post-doctoral) Research Fellow in Tribal Development of the Ministry of Welfare, Government of India. He has published numerous works like Administration for Rural Development in India; The Hill Korwa; The Korku Tribals; The Madia of Bhamragad; The Banjaras ; Political Anthropology and Tribal Exploitation, etc.

At present, Dr. Deogaonkar is working as Head, Department of Political Science at the Anand Niketan College, Warora (Maharashtra).

TRIBAL DEVELOPMENT PLANS

Implementation and Evaluation

S.G. Deogaonkar

CONCEPT PUBLISHING COMPANY PVT. LTD.
NEW DELHI-110059

ISBN : 978-81-7022-434-1

Edition 2020

Published and Printed by

Concept
Since 1974

Concept Publishing Company Pvt. Ltd.
A/15-16, Commercial Block, Mohan Garden,
New Delhi-110059 (INDIA)
T : +91 11 25351460, +91 11 25351794
E : publishing@conceptpub.com, *W* : www.conceptpub.com

FOREWORD

It was a pleasure and privilege to read the book based on the report prepared by Dr. Deogaonkar on the 'Implementation of the Tribal Sub-plan Schemes in the Primitive Tribal Areas of the Gadchiroli District of Maharashtra'.

The report is valuable in many respects. The geographical area selected for the study is one of the most backward (economically and socially) tribal pockets of this country where modernity has yet to reach. Dr. Deogaonkar has already done considerable work on the socio-cultural dimensions of this tribal society and hence is well conversant with almost all the dimensions of the life of the people here. Formulation of the problem and selection of the sample has been done systematically; field-work has been done in an honest manner and the results of the field-work have been presented without fear of the administration and with concern for the Tribals. The most important part of the report, of course, is the portion dealing with the evaluation and suggestions made by the author. In the present report Dr. Deogaonkar has reached a conclusion that the Tribals are willing to accept the new technology, methods and some schemes like commercial dairy development which was not in their culture. One is tempted to suggest Dr. Deogaonkar to take up a further study of impact of economic development on the culture of these tribal groups.

Dr. Deogaonkar deserves warm appreciation for the present addition to his already rich contribution to the studies on the tribal life. The book is highly recommended to all those interested in the tribal development.

Nagpur
26th Jan. 1991

S.V. KHANDEWALE
Dean, Faculty of Social Sciences,
Nagpur University, Nagpur

ACKNOWLEDGMENTS

I am extremely happy to place this book in the hands of my readers. It tries to evaluate the efforts for tribal development in general and the implementation of the Tribal sub-plan schemes in primitive tribal areas in particular in Maharashtra State. The Gadchiroli district in Maharashtra was known for its expansive forests with its inhabitants which was classified as a large primitive tribal group (socially and economically primitive) with a typical culture and way of life. Of late the district is known as a sensitive area due to increased Terrorist and Naxalite activity. The nexus between development and terrorism is a new dimension which attracts attention of administrators, politicians, social workers and all these who care for the unity and integrity of our country. It is hoped that the objective analysis of the implementation of the tribal development programmes and a dispassionate appraisal will help in furthering the development process and mitigating violence. Some perspectives for future are also given.

My thanks are due to the Tribal Development Department, Government of India, New Delhi for the National fellowship given by them which made this study possible. I must express my deep sense of gratitude to the Planning Commission for giving me an opportunity to place my views as Member of the Socio-Economic Group on S.C./S.T. for formulation of the Eighth Plan under their B.C. Division. The inter-action with other members of the Group also proved useful in sharing experiences.

I am thankful to Dr. P.S.K. Menon, Joint Director (Research) T.D.D. Min. of Welfare and Dr. D.K. Ray Dy. Director in the same Department for their encouragement and guidance. Dr. B.D. Sharma, Commissioner for S.C./S.T., has always been encouraging me in my research and welfare activities among tribals. I must thank him in encouraging me publishing the findings of this research project in the form of this book.

I am also thankful to the Government of Maharashtra, their officers for their cooperation and particularly the Tribal Research and Training Institute at Pune and its Director. Thanks are also due to the officers at the Nagpur Divisional Commissionerate level and in the Gadchiroli district as well as the officers at ITDPs in the District, Officers of the Forest Department and other Development Department were also helpful and deserve my gratitude.

Before I end this note I must mention the help and assistance given by my wife Dr. (Mrs.) Shailaja S. Deogaonkar in my work. Thanks are due to Shri Ashok Kumar Mittal of Concept Publishing Company for publishing this book.

S.G. DEOGAONKAR

CONTENTS

Foreword 5
Acknowledgments 7
List of Abbreviations 10
List of Tables 11

1. Introduction 13
2. The Madia-Gond: A Primitive Tribe 24
3. The Administration for Development 32
4. Implementation of Schemes 56
5. Screening of the Schemes Implemented 82
6. Attitudes and Opinions 141
7. Restructuring the Model 146
8. Tribal Culture and Development 156
9. Perspective for Tribal Development 161

Appendices
I. List of Beneficiaries and the benefits studied 171
II. List of 31 Villages under ITDP (Primitive Tribe), Bhamragad 185
III. List of Villages of Primitive Tribes in Bhamragad Area 186
IV. List of Villages covered under R.C. Bhamragad 187
V. A Model of Forestry-based Integrated Rural Development Programme 190

Bibliography 198
Map 199
Index 200

LIST OF ABBREVIATIONS

A.T.S.P.	Additional Tribal Sub-Plan.
B.I.L.T.	Ballarpur Industries Limited.
B.M.A.	Bench Mark Survey.
C.D.P.O.	Child Development Project Officer.
D.F.O.	Divisional Forest Officer.
D.R.D.A.	District Rural Development Agency.
I.C.D.S.	Integrated Child Development Scheme.
I.T.D.P.	Integrated Tribal Development Project.
L.B.P.	Lok Biradari Prakalpa
M.A.D.A.	Modified Area Development Approach.
M.S.E.B.	Maharashtra State Electricity Board.
M.S.T.D.C.	Maharashtra State Tribal Development Corporation.
Mini-M.A.D.A.	Mini-Modified Area Development Approach.
N.B.	Nucleus Budget.
O.T.S.P.	Outside Tribal Sub-Plan.
P.C.B.D.O.	Project-cum-Block Development Officer.
P.O.	Project Officer.
P.S.	Panchayat Samiti
P.W.D.	Public Works Department.
S.A.P.	Special Action Plan.
S.C.A.	Special Central Assistance.
T.D.O.	Tribal Development Officer.
T.S.P.	Tribal Sub-Plan.
Z.P.	Zilla Parishad.

LIST OF TABLES

1.1 Bhamragad – Schemes Implemented and Number of Benefits Studied Yearwise **22**

1.2 Etapalli – Schemes Implemented and Number of Benefits Studied Yearwise **23**

2.1 Families Settled in the Villages **31**

3.1 Districtwise Total and Tribal Population of Maharashtra State **45**

3.2 S.T. Population in Maharashtra in Three Decades **45**

3.3 Tribal Sub-Plan Area – Important Indicators of Maharashtra State **46**

3.4 Districtwise Tribal Population in Tribal Sub-plan Area (T.S.P. area) and Outside Tribal Sub-Plan Area (O.T.S.P. area) as per 1981 Census **46**

3.5 Total Number of Ashram Schools and Post-Basic Ashram-Schools in T.S.P. and O.T.S.P. area at the end of 1986-87 **47**

3.6 I.T.D.P.-wise Number of Villages/Towns/M.A.D.A. Pockets, (under Scheduled Area)/Mini M.A.D.A. pockets and A.T.S.P. areas of Maharashtra State **47**

3.7 Number of Villages covered under Scheduled Area (Tahsilwise)/ M.A.D.A. Pocket/Mini-M.A.D.A. Pocket/A.T.S.P. Area of Maharashtra State (1971 Census) **48**

3.8 I.T.D.P.-wise Scheduled Tribe Population covered under T.S.P./M.A.D.A., Pockets/Mini-M.A.D.A. Pockets/and A.T.S.P. areas of Maharashtra State as per 1981 Census **49**

3.9 Number of Villages, Total and Tribal Population covered under M.A.D.A. Pockets as per 1981 Census in Maharashtra position as on 1-4-1987 (Provisional) **50**

3.10 Total No. of Scheduled Tribe Families and those below poverty line in the Sub-plan Area of Maharashtra State **51**

3.11 District-wise Scheduled Tribe Families below Poverty Line (as per D.R.D.A. Survey, 1980) **51**

3.12 Total number of Scheduled Tribe families, landless Scheduled Tribe families with their percentages with total in Tribal Sub-Plan area of Maharashtra State **52**

3.13 Forest Areas in Maharashtra State (1980) **52**

3.14 Area Under Different Categories of Forest in Tribal Sub-Plan of Maharashtra State **53**
3.15 District-wise Primary Schools and Enrolment in Tribal Sub-Plan Area **54**
3.16 District-wise Number of Villages and Towns covered in M.A.D.A. Pockets, Mini-M.A.D.A. Pockets and A.T.S.P. area of Maharashtra State as on 1-4-1987 **55**
4.1 Statement of Schemes taken as for the Benefit of Primitive Bada Madia Tribe of Bhamragad under *Nucleus Budget* for the Year *1981-82* **68**
4.2 Expenditure Under Nucleus Budget for the Year 1982-83 **70**
4.3 Expenditure Under Nucleus Budget for the Year 1983-84 **71**
4.4 Expenditure Under Nucleus Budget For the Year 1984-85 **72**
4.5 Expenditure Under Nucleus Budget for the Year 1985-86 **73**
4.6 Nucleus Budget Allotment — Sanctioned Rs. 3 Lakhs for 1986-87 **74**
4.7 Special Central Assistance — 1982-83 **76**
4.8 Special Central Assistance — 1983-84 **77**
4.9 Special Central Assistance — 1984-85 **78**
4.10 Special Central Assistance — 1985-86 **79**
4.11 Provision for 1986-87 Special Central Assistance **80**
4.12 Statement showing the Yearwise Expenditure Under Nucleus Budget: From 1981-82 to 1985-86 **81**
4.13 Statement showing the Yearwise Expenditure Under Special Central Assistance from 1982-83 to 1985-86 **81**
5.1 Schemes implemented through grants to Lok-Biradari Prakalpa, Hemalkasa **98**
5.2 Information Regarding Oil-engine Pumps **121**
5.3 Information Regarding Electric Motor Pumps **122**
5.4 Action taken of Applications Received for Oil-pumps and Electric Pumps during 1986-87 **123**
5.5 Supply of Electric/Oil Pumps under 20 Point Programme during 1986-87 **124**
5.6 Statement showing expenditure on distribution of Uniforms to School Children and average per-uniform expenditure **129**
9.1 Details of Special Action Plan for Gadchiroli District **163**

1

INTRODUCTION

The Preamble to the Indian Constitution promises Justice–social, economic and political and upholds Liberty, Equality and Fraternity as lofty ideals for all the citizens. In Part IV of the Constitution a just and egalitarian socio-economic order is promised (sooner or later) through democratic, socialist planning. Article 23 bestows a Right Against Exploitation to those brethren who have been the victims of social environment for centuries. These principles and promises in our Constitution earned acclaim for us as a nation in the world.

Under such specific provisions of our Constitution and also as per the policy accepted by the Government of India, we as a Nation are committed to strive hard for the upliftment of the weaker sections of our society which includes the tribal population amounting to seven per cent of the total population. Special schemes, administrative structures, specific financial provisions etc. have been made since planning started and much has been said and done. The primitive tribes have their typical problems arising, among other things from their typical physical as well as socio-cultural environment. Inaccessibility of the areas, absence of all weather roads, a primitive type of agricultural economy and ignorance, blind-faith and superstition and a general-fear — complex perpetuating secluded life also adds to the backwardness. Since Planning started, special attention has been paid to such tribal pockets, however as the general approach was found to be inadequate for the development of such primitive tribal pockets sub-plans within the plans were envisaged. Such Tribal Sub-plans were carefully formulated adopting principles and approaches flexible enough for facing and solving known as well as not-known problems of these areas and populations. The Integrated Tribal Development Programmes were supposed to give fillip to the development efforts and the Tribal Sub-plans provided the necessary administrative and financial support tailor-made for each project area.

In Maharashtra the Government specified two tribal communities as 'primitive' viz. the *Katkaris* from the Thane district and the *Madia-Gonds* from the Gadchiroli district. However, the Katkaris were considered only as economically backward while the Madia-Gonds inhabiting the Etapalli tahsil of the Gadchiroli district were considered primitive — both socially and economically.

In 1974-75 the Tribal Sub-Plan was formulated in Maharashtra State, however the actual implementation started in 1975-76. It was thought that the new infrastructures created, techniques adopted and actual schemes implemented should be evaluated with a view to find out the actual impact on the tribal beneficiaries and to serve as a feed-back to planners.

The broad hypotheses were as under:

(1) The Tribal Sub-Plan (TSP) schemes have been implemented in the area under study and the new structures are now firmly rooted.
(2) The Madia-Gond (primitive) tribals in the area have been economically benefited as a result of the schemes under the T.S.P.
(3) The tribals have responded favourably to the schemes under the T.S.P.
(4) The social life of these tribals has also changed towards better living as a result of the schemes implemented under the T.S.P.

The study envisaged to consider some group beneficiary schemes like Ashram/Residential schools, the Integrated Child Development Schemes and other follow-up schemes if any. However, the main emphasis of the study was at the micro-level where individual tribal beneficiaries were supposed to receive the benefit. Particularly the schemes under the Nucleus Budget (N.B.) and Special Central Assistance (S.C.A.) were to be studied as they are supposed to be prepared considering the specific problems of the beneficiaries and have an element of specificness and flexibility. They form an important component of the Tribal Sub-Plan approach and treatment.

As this research project commenced in August 1985 and was to run through 1985-86 and 1986-87, it was decided to study the schemes implemented during the financial years 1984-85, 1985-86 and schemes which were being implemented during 1986-87 for which data/latest facts etc. were available, were also covered. Beneficiaries under schemes during 1982-83 and 1983-84 were covered on a small scale because the concerned offices were unable to find-out and provide the detailed records and names of all beneficiaries.

Before proceeding further it is also essential to take an overview of the work already done on the problem.

An Overview of Research Work already Carried Out in the Area

The Tribal Research and Training Institute (Pune) of the Government of Maharashtra had undertaken an 'Evaluation Study of Integrated Tribal Development Project — Gadchiroli-I, Etapalli', the report of which (cyclostyled) was brought out in November 1985. This study covers three Panchayat Samiti areas viz. Aheri, Etapalli (which includes Special I.T.D.P. — at Bhamragad) and Sironcha, and relates to the financial years 1981-82, 1982-83 and 1983-84 (The separate Gadchiroli district came into existence w.e.f. 26-8-1982.)

As mentioned at pp. 44 and 45 of the Report of the said Project, the methodology for evaluation was based on 'case studies' wherein (some schemes were studied as 'case studies'), the main objective of these case studies being to (see para 5.1 of the Report) 'study the location of educational/public health institutions, the status of facilities available, inclination of people to facilities, to assess the administrative work of the institutions, status of roads, and to know the features of different, schemes implemented under forest sector'.

While indicating the constraints under which the Tribal Research and Training Institute of the Government of Maharashtra (T.R.T.I.) carried out the Project, the following find to mention here (see p. 17 of the said Report):

(i) the number of schemes and volume of work (for the study project).
(ii) time at the disposal (of the Institute).
(iii) lack of manpower (with the Institute).
(iv) geographical mobility of the I.T.D.P. area.
(v) requisite information not received within specified time (from concerned offices in the field) and consequent frequency of visits of the T.R.T.I. officers to the area.
(vi) . . . most of the records (in the field offices) were incomplete. (Brackets added)

Due to these constraints, the Report states, it was not possible for the T.R.T.I. to cover all sectors of the tribal people and hence they selected the schemes from the following Departments namely:

(1) Forest — Two schemes (covering ten individual beneficiaries each as detailed below).
(2) Education — Group benefit schemes.
(3) Public Health.
(4) Roads and Communication.

So far as the schemes under Education, Public Health and Roads and Communication are concerned the Report produces data of the physical targets achieved, supplied by the concerned functional offices of the respective Departments. However under Forest, ten individual beneficiaries under two schemes of the Forest Department have been contacted and studied.

As detailed in para 5.3 (p. 45) of the said report, Government Primary Schools, Hostels, Balwadis, Z.P. School and a Private run school were studied. In public health schemes, Primary Health Centres; the Christian Missions' Hospital and Lok-Biradari (a private hospital) were also studied under I.T.D.P. These were all schemes where beneficiaries were in a group and/or in an institutional form.

Individual tribal beneficiaries were studied in the 'case studies' under Forest Department where two specific schemes with individuals as beneficiaries were studied and here the beneficiaries were interviewed. The names of the schemes and number of beneficiaries are given below:

	Scheme	*Number of individual beneficiaries interviewed*
(a)	Supply of Bullock pairs/carts	Five
(b)	Equipment	Five

Thus in this evaluation study total ten individual beneficiaries were studied. In addition Christian Missionaries at the christian 'Assissi Hospital' at Allapalli and Dr. Prakash Amte at Lokbiradari, Hemalkasa were also interviewed.

Thus, the report is a brilliant document giving details about the administrative machinery for I.T.D.P. at various levels and about the various schemes under it as envisaged by the planners, valuable statistics from office records indicating the physical targets achieved and most valuable suggestions based on the study.

The above evaluation report of the Tribal Research and Training Institute, Pune, which is marked as 'For office use only' is the only previous literature on the topic and area.

Coverage and Methodology

The Madia-Gonds which is classified as a primitive tribe is spread in the thick forests of the Etapalli, Panchayat Samiti area. The Panchayat Samiti as well as the Tahsil headquarters are at Etapalli. The Project office of the I.T.D.P. Primitive Tribes Project is at Bhamragad and originally consists of 31 villages (out of which 10 are barren) and some more were later added to it to swell the number to 61 out of which only 57 are inhabited. Though this is the model carried out for the purposes of the developmental in-puts for Primitive Tribes Area, anthropologically and historically the Madia-Gond tribes' habitat consists even of the village around Etapalli. The *Pattis* or administrative units of the erstwhile Aheri Zamindari (under the Maharaja of Aheri who is still revered by the Madia-Gonds in the whole area under reference) consisted of the four *Pattis* viz. *Laheri Patti, Venusagar Patti, Jaravandi Patti,* and *Ghat Patti,* each headed by a *Sendhia,*[1] which at present includes the Madia-Gond villages from both the Etapalli and Bhamragad Blocks bracketed under the Etapalli Panchayat Samiti. Even considering the food, shelter and clothing habits, and the general stage of acculturation. The men and women in the Etapalli area are still 'Primitive' though they have more and better opportunities of communication with outsides. During the past 7-8 years the road between Etapalli and Allapalli — Aheri is good and negotiable throughout twelve months.

The Project Officer for the Etapalli I.T.D. Project office area is usually senior to the Bhamragad (Primitive Tribes) Project Officer, and the Block-staff for both the T.D. Blocks is also located at

1. Deogaonkar, S.G. *The Madia of Bhamragad*, Concept Publishing Co., 1982, New Delhi, p. 15.

Etapalli. The communication and contact of officers is more in this part as compared to Bhamragad and ahead. However, the fact remains that the tribal life in the Madia-Gond villages surrounding Etapalli is also primitive and hence as a support to the field-investigation-work done in the special 'Primitive Tribes' project, the beneficiaries from a few Madia-Gond villages around Etapalli were also studied. In all ten villages were covered from this area.

Methodology

(i) *Sample-size*

The Government of Maharashtra has termed the Bhamragad I.T.D. Project area as I.T.D.P. (Primitive Tribes) specially at Bhamragad. In all, 113 villages are covered under the Bhamragad I.T.D.P. out of which 17 villages are *Masahat* i.e. uninhabited (as per 1981 Census) (See Appendix IV). From the inhabited 96 villages, 31 villages were included under I.T.D.P. (Primitive Tribes), Bhamragad out of which 10 villages are uninhabited (See Appendix II). Hence, only 21 villages remained which included 19 villages with 100 per cent tribal population mostly (Madia-Gonds) and only one with 86 per cent tribal population. Out of these twenty villages, seven villages were selected for the purpose of this investigation. The Government of Maharashtra further added villages to the Projects, bringing the total number of inhabited villages to 57. (See Appendix III). In all, 22 villages were selected in which 18 are from the 57 listed and four from the I.T.D.P., Bhamragad and 163 beneficiaries under various schemes were personally contacted and verifications made on the spot. From the 10 villages from I.T.D.P., Etapalli area 41 beneficiaries were covered. Thus the total number of beneficiaries covered was 204. (See Appendix I for the list of beneficiaries village-wise). Apart from beneficiaries, many other tribals from the villages which included non-beneficiaries were also contacted, their total number exceeding hundred. Their consensus on the schemes was found useful.

(ii) *Selection of Villages/Beneficiaries*

The selection of villages for the purpose largely depended upon the lists of beneficiaries supplied by different departments, in which names of villages of beneficiaries were supplied. From among the villages whose names appeared in those lists, villages were selected depending upon —

(a) accessibility of village (development depends upon communication).

   (i) Villages on the main forest road,
   (ii) Villages away from the main forest road,
   (iii) Secluded and inaccessible villages. (Please see the list of villages covered on the following page)

(b) varieties of benefits — to individuals as well as to group/community — given in villages. Broadly, this was a purposive sampling.

Lists of beneficiaries during the years under study were obtained from the concerned offices and then field-visits were planned. Beneficiaries under different schemes implemented from the village(s), were selected for study. Almost all beneficiaries who had not left the village and who were not out of station were contacted.

(iii) *Tools/Methods of Investigation*

In most of the villages the contacts were successful. With the help of local *Gaita* (*Patel*) the individuals were located and free associational interviews conducted.

Participant observation method was also followed and it could be possible due to the researcher's personal rapport in the area.

Most of the tribals are scared of a written schedule being canvassed in their presence. Hence a small format about beneficiaries was kept ready and verifications made by visiting the hut, farm, well, bodi etc. on the spot. Later, coming to *Ghotul* general discussions were held with the beneficiaries and local community leaders. Group benefits were also seen and examined in person and views of villagers obtained.

In a few cases where the beneficiaries agreed to respond to a written schedule, elaborate interviews based on schedule were conducted.

Thus, field-investigation work was based on personal visits to the selected villages, from the project area; participant observation, personal contacts with the tribal beneficiaries under various schemes implemented, physical verification of the benefits if any, and estimation of the reaction of the beneficiaries to the benefit, schemes and/or of the operators of the schemes were estimated. This work was done personally by the undersigned. The researcher travelled by bus, and also hired jeep as per requirement and visited even the remotest villages. In some cases the vehicle could not be taken and a few Kilometers distance had to be negotiated by trekking. The team included the following persons:

(1) Ku. Nanda Kangalrao Kulsange — a Gond girl knowing the area and dialect.
(2) Shri Gogga Khola Pungati — A Madia Gayata (Patel) of village Gotpadi.
(3) Shri Karve Doly Parsa — A Madia Tribal from Gotpadi.
(4) Shri Bodanga Kando — A Madia of village Krishnar.
(5) Shri Mallu Alias Manohar Ganda Hichami — Madia from village Krishnar.
(6) Shri D.J. Warwade (a Tribal) Teacher in Zilla Parishad School at Gotpadi (knowing the Madia dialect).

As the research fellow himself knows the area, the people and the dialect the work was facilitated, however the persons from the above team assisted while moving in different tracts and visiting villages. We stayed in *Ghotuls*, huts and squatted on ground with tribals. The local *Gayatas* (Patels/headmen of village) seemed to be extremely eager to help and hence work in respective villages was facilitated. It is interesting to note that in many cases when we moved out and went to other village the beneficiaries who were not in village came all the way to meet us in the next village to narrate their problems and complaints. Photographs were also taken by the author.

Villages Covered in the Study

(I) *Bhamragad I.T.D.P. (Primitive Tribes Area)*

Category I – Inaccessible – extremely difficult to reach– cut-off during rainy season.

(1) Aldandi (2) Bangadi (3) Binagunda (4) Bodange (5) Gundenhod (6) Kuvvakodi (7) Nelgunda (8) Turremarka.

Category II – On *Kuccha* forest roads, through circutous routes – away from the main road, deep in forest.

(1) Arewada (2) Gongwada (3) Goptadi (4) Hiddur (5) Hitapadi (6) Juvvi (7) Kiyar (8) Koyar (9) Murangal.

Category III – On the main road (*Kuccha* Forest Road – now some parts are tarred).

(1) Bhamragad (Tola) (2) Dhodraj (3) Hemalkasa (4) Laheri (5) Malampoddur.

ITDP, Etapalli Area

Category I — Nil. All villages accessible.
Category II — (1) Chokhewada (2) Dumme (3) Geda (4) Javelli (5) Krishnar (6) Pandhewahi.
Category III — (1) Etappalli (2) Jarawandi (3) Kandli (4) Kasansur.

Financial Years

The years for which the benefits under various schemes were covered under this study included – 1982-83, 1983-84, 1984-85, 1985-86, and 1986-87. But most of the schemes/beneficiaries covered were from the years 1984-85 and 1985-86 and 1986-87 because most of the concerned offices supplied data and lists of beneficiaries for that period. The figures and lists of beneficiaries supplied by the relevant operating Departments formed the basis for this verification work. However, grievances, complaints, and reactions of others and of the non-beneficiaries were also listened to and noted.

Operating Officers

The various agencies/offices under whom the schemes under study were operated included:

(1) Project Officer, I.T.D.P. (Primitive Tribes) specially at Bhamragad.
(2) Project Officer, I.T.D.P., Etapalli.
(3) The Maharashtra State Tribal Development Corporation. (Sub-Regional Manager's office), Aheri.

(4) Tribal Development Officer, Aheri.
(5) Deputy Director, Animal Husbandry/Distt. Animal Husbandry Officer, Gadchiroli.
(6) The C.D.P.O., I.C.D.S., Etapalli.
(7) Divisional Forest Officer, Bhamragad Division, Allapalli.
(8) Executive Engineer, P.W.D., Allapalli.
(9) P.C.B.D.O., Panchayat Samiti, Etapalli.
(10) Tribal Areas Research Project (Punjabrao Krishi Vidyapeeth, Akola) at Aheri.
(11) Some other Departments like Education Technical Education, Fisheries, Agriculture, Public Health, etc. and other private/voluntary agencies like the Ballarpur Industries Ltd., and the Lok Biradari Prakalpa, Hemalkasa, B.A.J.S.S. etc.

I.T.D.P. (Primitive Tribe)

TABLE 1.1: Bhamragad — Schemes Implemented and Number of Benefits Studied Yearwise

Scheme	1982-83	83-84	84-85	85-86	86-87	Total
Tiles for roofing	0	3	25	10	11	49
Repairs to hut — Roofing Tiles	—	—	1	2	—	3
Pair of bullocks	—	—	25	6	2	33
Bullock carts	—	1	5	7	1	14
Pair of bullocks & carts	—	1	10	3	1	15
Cycle shop	—	—	2	—	—	2
Grocery shop	—	—	—	1	—	1
Vegetable shop	—	—	—	1	—	1
Oil Engines	2	1	4	1	1	9
Ploughing of land by Tractor	—	—	—	5	—	5
Training in Animal-Husbandry + cow, calf & Goat.	2	—	—	6	15	23
Milk-can/Kettle	—	—	—	5	4	9
Cycle	—	—	—	—	6	6
Earth work implements	1	—	—	4	—	5
Brick-making (81-82)	—	—	—	1	—	1
Sewing Machines 1	—	1	—	—	—	2
Trip to Nagpur and other places.	—	—	—	—	6	6
Utensils, Blankets etc.	—	—	1	—	1	2
Broom purchase	—	—	—	—	1	1
Metal work training	1	—	—	—	—	1
Community Marriage of Madias	—	—	—	—	1	1
Total Number of benefits studied						189

I.T.D.P.,

TABLE 1.2: Etapalli — Schemes Implemented and Number of Benefits Studied Yearwise

Scheme			1982-83	83-84	84-85	85-86	86-87	Total
Tiles for roofing			—	—	—	10	—	10
Grocery/Manery shop			—	—	—	1	—	1
Vegetable shop			—	—	—	1	—	1
General Stores			—	—	—	3	—	3
Gobar-gas plant			3	1	2	6	—	12
	(78-79)	(80-81)						
Oil Engines	1	1	—	1	2	—	—	5
Electric pump	—	—	—	—	—	—	1	1
Goat keeping	—	—	—	—	—	1	—	1
Poultry	—	—	—	—	—	1	—	1
Training in English Typing			—	—	—	1	—	1
Sewing Machines		—	—	—	*3	2	—	5
Total Number of benefits studied								41

* Scheme implemented by Punjabrao Krishi Vidyapeeth, Akola through its Tribal Area Research Project, Aheri Centre.

2

THE MADIA-GOND: A Primitive Tribe*

The erstwhile – Chandrapur district in Maharashtra State lies between 18° and 20° North and 78° and 81° East. It had an area of 25,641 square kilometres of which urban areas account for 103.3 sq.km and rural areas for 25,532.7 sq.km. The district had six tahsils viz., Chandrapur, Warora, Brahmapuri, Gadchiroli, Sironcha and Rajura, out of which the Sironcha tahsil was the largest in area. Since August 1982 the new Gadchiroli district has been created with Headquarters at Gadchiroli, which covers the old Gadchiroli and Sironcha tahsils. Sironcha tahsil also is divided into three tahsils viz. Sironcha, Aheri and Etapalli but, are under one Sub-Divisional Officer i.e. S.D.O., Sironcha with headquarters at Aheri. Etapalli tahsil covers the area under study and has its headquarters at Etapalli. It is this tahsil which incorporates the thick forest which is well-known for three things viz. the best teak-wood, natural beauty with big rivers, hills and wild-life and lastly the primitive tribals viz., the Madia-Gond. The Etapalli Panchayat Samiti is the administrative unit which covers two T.D. Blocks viz. Etapalli and Bhamragad, the major population of which consists of these tribals. This region, south of Chandrapur is, full of almost virgin land and the best developed forests are found in this area covered under Allapalli and Bhamragad Forest Divisions. Along the Indravati, Bandia and Pranhita rivers occur almost pure teak-tree ranges. The other common trees are *Suria* (or Indian Ironwood tree), *Sal, Rohan, Tendu, Salai, Mahua, Char, Semul, Tad* etc. The whole area has hills spreading up to the border touching Bastar (M.P.). The soil is alluvial loam, gravelly

---

* This account is taken from the author's book '*The Madia of Bhamragad*' which is based on his own anthropological research on the Madia tribe.

course, and somewhat sandy.

The Gond Tribe

Among the many tribes in the Gadchiroli district, the Gonds were a dominant race for centuries, spreading far beyond the district. The Gonds in this area can be broadly divided into four endogamous sub-tribes or groups: the Raj-Gond, the Madia-Gond, Dhurve and Khatulwar Gond. But the two main sects of the Gonds in the Sironcha tahsil of the district are the Raj-Gond and the Madia-Gond, among whom the bulk of the population is divided. The Madia inhabit the wilder tracts of what was once known as the Aheri Zamindari area and their villages are situated deep in the jungles. A few Raj-Gonds are found in these wilder tracts and hilly areas e.g. in Hindewada, Arewada etc. 'Madia' means a 'forest-dweller', and they don't like leaving their habitat. *Pradhans* who are known as minstrels of the Gonds are also seen dwelling in some villages like Arewada, Gongwada etc. The Gonds consider them inferior in rank and status. The Govari, believed to be of Gond extraction are found in many Gond villages, and are primarily a grazier caste. Zarey or Zaramins are also sighted notably in villages like Gollaguda, Arewada etc. Otankars who are traditional gold (actually silver) smiths are located in Koyanguda, Kiyar and in a few other villages.

These tribes, though very rich in their own traditional culture, are still considered as being at a low stage of acculturation.

The Bhamragad area which is the area of habitat of the Madia is not communicable for all the twelve months in the year. Due to *kuccha* forest roads, communication is cut-off with the first monsoon showers. Big rivers like Parlakota, Indravati, Bandiya and Pamal-Gautam (or Nibra) are without bridges. The temporary bridges (rafts) built are washed-off in the rainy season. Vehicles cannot ply on forest roads except for jeeps – that too occasionally. People have to go on foot and use country ferries on the rivers. Since 1980, the road between Allapalli and Etapalli has been repaired as a result of which State Transport buses ply throughout the year. However the area between Etapalli and Bhamragad and the villages lying ahead of Bhamragad up to Kuvvakodi are still cut-off for six to seven months from the neighbouring areas in the tahsil. The confluence of the rivers Parlakota, Indravati and Pamal-Gautam at Bhamragad presents a picturesque sight.

There are many villages which are deep in the forest and can be approached only on foot. Some villages like Aldandi, Binagunda, Bangadi, Turremarka, Kuvvakodi etc. are on the hills and one has to climb hills for reaching such villages. Only a skilled driver can risk the negotiating of these roads by a jeep.

The Madia-Gonds

The Madia are sub-divided into two groups viz., the Hill or Bada-Madia and the Chota-Madia depending upon their traditional places of domicile. The Bada-Madia live in the far off forests on hills and is relatively in more primitive condition. They do not mix with their counterparts in the plains and are more orthodox. The Chota-Madia who must have migrated long back to the plains and the riversides show signs of change and are more acculturised. The Bada- and Chota-Madia are almost like two castes and eating and marriage relationship between these two groups are tabooed.

The Bada-Madia living on the hills near and ahead of Bhamragad and Laheri are mostly concentrated in certain villages in the Bhamragad Block mainly at Laheri, Bangadi, Gundenhod, Poerkothi, Hiddur, Dirangi, Binagunda, Kuvakodi etc. Chota-Madia is mainly found at Kiyar, Murangal, Gotpadi, Tadpari, Bodange, Koyar, Puswara, Laheri, Juvvi, Hodri Gollagunda, Morametta, Parainar, Kawande, Poyarkothi and Krusinar etc. At places like Laheri and many other villages there is a mixed population consisting of both the Madia. The Bada Madia are traditionally shifting cultivators. Many families have now been settled. However they still practise it on hill slopes ahead of Gundenhod.

Youth dormitories are found in the institution of *Ghotuls* of the Madia.

The People

The Madia are of medium height-about five feet to five and a half feet, of medium build, and have a dark complexion. Their skin colour ranges between moderate black to dark tan and they have a shiny skin. Their noses are a bit flat on the tapering side and they have bright black eyes. They keep their hair long and some of them possess typically curly hair. They cut their hair near the neck and may shave the front part of the head i.e. 3″ -4″ above the forehead in a semi-circle. Every Madia shaves his beard regularly and also grooms his hair properly. Hence shabby-looking Madia are rare. They have good muscles and a solid torso.

The Madia women are about the same height and complexion with a smart face and look, and obviously more intelligent than the men-folk. They are well-built and have full-grown breasts which are always kept uncovered – specially by married girls and women – as per their traditions. Without any mechanical devices and beauty aids their limbs show an artistic disposition which is a result of hard work and nature care. Their hair is long, always dressed by hand-made wooden combs and kept in place by hair-pins etc. They keep themselves very clean and are always very joyous-especially the younger lot. Fond of ornaments, they use profuse silver ornaments and glass or stone beads etc. to cover their necks.

Both men and women are scantily clad and the men normally wear a loin cloth or a strip of cloth in between the legs – 'a *langoti*'. These days the younger people use underpants, preferably black in colour. They generally don't cover the part above the waist except in occasional cases when they come in contact with outsiders. Even a person of the rank of Chairman Panchayat Samiti would remove his shirt and *dhoti* immediately after going home. A black cap, indicating alignment with their Maharaja's party is occasionally used by some Madia.

Women use a small towel-like loin cloth around their waists and keep the portion above the waist completely bare, Previously – and even now – they used to wear a triangular piece of cloth in between their legs – like a fig-leaf, but nowadays they cover it with a waist cloth wrapped around the waist which is usually short.

Rarely, the women use the *lugda* (nine yard sarees) and when they do, they do not cover their breasts with it except in a few cases and that too only before a stranger. They like white-coloured sarees; and for married girls or women covering breasts is tabooed. After solemnisation of the marriage, water is poured over the heads of the bride and bride-groom and then their clothes are changed. Afterwards she is not allowed to cover he breasts as a mark of her being a wife. Unmarried girls who are a bit modernised are now wearing blouses and coloured five metre sarees but this also continues only up to marriage. If we go to the areas which lie deeper in the forests, even teenage and marriageable girls use only waist cloth.

Children are normally naked and only those going to school may be seen with clothes. One must understood that scanty clothes are not necessarily a sign of poverty; it is their way of life and a tradition. A women sporting a thick silver-belt (*Kamarpatta*) around her waist and many silver necklaces would use only a loin cloth.

Compared to the men, the Madia women are more active, and hardworking and have good strength. They toil hard on farms and even plough the fields without a pair of bullocks or with one bullock on one side of the yoke. They dig earth, pound rice, grind, build huts, fell trees and do almost everything for the household. Thus, in strength as well as managing capacity, they compare fairly well with men, or even surpass them. Hence a woman or a wife is an economic asset to the family. That is the reason why polygamy could continue without damaging the economic life of the family.

Men are strong, calm and hardworking but are lazy as compared to women. They work on farms or do manual labour as forest labourers. But on many occasions one finds them roaming around the forest for hunting-their traditional source of livelihood and food, which, these days is mostly a futile exercise. The Madia thus whiles away time. They worship *Persapen* (Bada Deo), Goddess Ankali and many local Gods. *Pujas* (*Pandums*) and festivals on various occasions are common. Dussera and Holi are important festivals. At all the festivals and ceremonies, worship, eating, drinking and dancing is common.

They lead a real community life and have honest relations based on equality of status. There is no exploitation amongst their own men and the Gayatas and Panchas settle quarrels, marital issues, divorces etc. Marriages are by free consent and brideprice is in vogue.

Ghotul is a community hut at the centre of each village where, traditionally teen-age boys and girls come together, mix freely, dance and choose their life partners.

Food and Eating Habits

Traditionally they are rice-eaters. They also grow maize, minor millets like *kusari, kutaki* etc. They prepare a semi liquid soup from rice called 'ambil' which is common in their daily food. They are mainly non-vegetarians and eat meat. They eat almost all animals and birds including reptiles. Even crows, sparrows, snakes are killed and eaten. Big red-ants are dried and eaten which was a very popular substitute for salt – a rare commodity for them until recent years. But, in general, animals and birds in this area are scarce so that they cannot rely on the fauna as their routine food. Even when they get it, the quantity is very small.

They eat *mahua* flowers and drink toddy and *gorga* (drawn from the *gorga* tree which is a fan-palm). Toddy is consumed in large quantities specially when they work hard on farms or as labourers, and it serves as a food-drink as well as a beverage. *Mahua* wine is prepared only during festivals or marriages and consumed collectively.

These days, in the courtyard, beans, cucumbers or pumpkins and grown and banana trees are also coming up. Some fruits like mangoes, custard apple *(Sitaphal)*, *amla* etc. are also available in the forests, but they usually don't eat fruits and vegetables and such fruit-trees are wasted.

The Madia keep buffaloes, cows, goats etc. and are fond of cattle; but they do not milk the cows or buffaloes. They are against milking the cattle and never drink milk or eat milk products. Their traditional superstition persists that if they milk the cows, blood would come out along with it and the calf as well as the cow would die. If some person starts milking a cow or a buffalo then he is obstructed and they go against him. Consequently Madia men, women and even their children don't use milk or milk products and are denied animal proteins. An outsider has to be contented with the decoction of tea devoid of milk. Even if they milk the animals it is for others and they don't drink milk or eat milk products.

The Madia grow tobacco in their courtyards for personal consumption. They eat and chew tobacco and use *tendu* leaves to prepare *bidis*. In the minor forest produce plucking of *tendu* leaves is an important occupation, they get wages for picking it as labourers for private contractors or the Forest Department. Collection of honey, myrobalans, gum and *mahua* flowers during the flowering season are pet pursuits in which women and small children are experts. Fishing is very common. In the tanks and lakes, and in the big rivers flowing through the forest they catch fish and at times get very big mammals. Big fish, eight to ten feet in length are also found in big rivers like Bandia and Indravati. Crocodiles are also occasionally obtained in these rivers. During and immediately after the rains they catch fish in small ditches around the village or in small *nullas,* rivulets, ponds etc.

They store paddy, seeds of beans, and even dried pieces of meat. The Madia also eat the roots and stems of certain trees. They mainly boil their food before eating. At times only roasting is sufficient. Long back they used to eat raw meat but these days it is roasted or cooked. Rice is boiled and cooked before eating. But this is done only on occasions. A soup of rice with eighty per cent water i.e. *ambil* is more common. Earthenware pots are used for storage and cooking which are prepared by local artisans. Thanks to communication with roving traders and merchants, 'German' (German silver as it is popularly known) utensils i.e. aluminium utensils are very common almost through all parts of their area. They use fire-wood and have a fire kindled all the day and night in their homes. It is never extinguished. Thus they don't need match-sticks. Some Madias can also kindle fire by rubbing wood or stones together. Fire has a very important role not only in their kitchens but as illumination and in all other aspects of their life. They do not use kerosene and kerosene lamps.

Drinking water is not easily available in some villages. Very few villages have wells in or around the village. They bring water from *nullas* or rivers which are far away from the village. Water is not pure but contaminated with minerals like mica or other soluble minerals hard to digest and secretions of roots of plants which are dangerous to health.

Settlement of Shifting Cultivators

As stated earlier, the Madia and particularly the Bada or Hill Madia practised shifting cultivation called *'Penda'*. On the slopes of the Laheri hills they used to cut forest before summer, allow the logs to dry, then burn it and after the first showers of rain sow seeds by broadcast method. Ploughing was traditionally tabooed the reason being, they should not use plough on the mother earth.

The Government of Maharashtra had a scheme of settling shifting cultivators by bringing them on plains and giving land, huts, utensils, bullocks, etc. thus 146 families were settled as shown in Table 2.1:

TABLE 2.1: Families Settled in the Villages

Year	Names of the villages	Name of the Tribes	No. of families	Total population
1	2	3	4	5
1959-60	Koyar	Chhota-	13	79
	Murangal	Madia	12	62
1960-61	Laheri	Bada Madia	5	86
	Bangadi		11	53
	Gundenhod		9	59
1961-62	Gotpadi	Chhota Madia	25	94
1962-63	Poerkuti	Bada Madia	25	102
1963-64	Tadpari	-do-	15	66
	Bedange	Chhota Madia	10	50
1964-65	Hiddur	Bada Madia	10	61
	Koyar	Chhota Madia	4	
	Murangal	-do-	4	
	Bodange	-do-	3	
	TOTAL		146	692

Literacy percentage ranges between 1 to 5 per cent and in case of women it is almost nil. Educational facilities were negligible and language posed an important hurdle. Health problems were rampant due to ignorance, superstitions and absence of hospitals/doctors etc. Due to virtual seclusion and absence of development-oriented attitude in their traditional leaders, these tribals were kept away from the mainstream of development. Primitive and/or traditional methods of cultivation, chronic indebtedness and exploitation by traders, money-lenders etc. added to their misery. It was on this background that innovative models for their development had to be planned.

3

THE ADMINISTRATION FOR DEVELOPMENT

The Policy and the Machinery for Tribal Development

A. *New Deal for Tribal Development*

The approach and strategy for tribal development was comprehensively reviewed on the eve of the Fifth Five Year Plan. The Shilu Ao Committee appointed by the Planning Commission during the Fourth Plan had already concluded that T.D. Block, as it finally got evolved, was an inadequate frame for tackling the complex problem of tribal development. A fresh look at the tribal scene gave a new lead to the effort. It became obvious that solutions must differ depending upon the situations in terms of resources, people, social constraints, infrastructural development, local priorities etc. Similarly it was recognised that the approach and strategy of tribal development has to be quite distinct for areas of tribal concentration and for areas with dispersed tribal populations. When area development plans are prepared the backward regions in general and the tribal regions in particular must be given significance and where tribal population is predominant, investment in infrastructural development also becomes an element in tribal development. Thus the concept of 'area development with focus on tribal development' was evolved.

Some tribal communities like the Madia-Gonds or the Abhujmaries the Ongo, the Bondo, who largely depend on food-gathering and hunting and are at an earlier stage of economic development were identified as primitive tribal communities. The need for a very flexible approach towards the development plans of such communities was recognised.

In pursuance of the above approach evolved on the eve of the

Fifth Plan, a comprehensive programme of development was prepared, in the first stage, for areas of tribal concentration. The programme for primitive tribal communities was also given a high priority and specific schemes were drawn up for them. It was, however, decided that intensive development of dispersed tribal communities will be taken up in the second phase.

All areas with more than 50 per cent tribal population have been treated as predominantly tribal areas. Separate plans have been prepared for these areas, which are known as 'tribal sub-plans'. In determining the population percentage of tribals in an area, the industrial and urban enclaves have been excluded. A tribal development block has been taken as the smallest unit for inclusion in the new programme. A group of blocks, which generally comprise a tahsil, has been taken as the basic unit for planning and development of the new tribal development programme. The unit is now known as Integrated Tribal Development Project (I.T.D.P.).

The 'Integrated' Approach

The draft Five Year Pan (1978-83) described the sub-plan approach as follows:

For the first time, an integrated sub-plan approach for tribal development was adopted during the Fifth Five Year Plan. Keeping in view the past experience of area development through Tribal Development Blocks, a new strategy was evolved to formulate separate sub-plans for areas of tribal concentration. These sub-plans continue to operate in 16 States and 2 Union Territories. About 2/3rd of the tribal population in the country is estimated to be covered by these sub-plans.

The broad objectives of the Tribal Sub-Plans are:

(i) to narrow the gap between the levels of development of tribal areas and other areas and

(ii) to improve the quality of life of the tribal communities. To achieve these objectives, elimination of exploitation of tribals in land alienation, indebtedness, bonded labour, mal-practices in exchange of agricultural and forest produce etc. was given the priority in Fifth Plan. Excise and forest policies were reviewed and suitable measures taken to end exploitation in tribal areas. In development programmes, priority was given to agriculture and allied sectors, irrigation facilities and forest-based and other industries. Infrastructure like roads and rural electrification was linked with the economic programmes. Agriculture programmes were oriented so as to provide increased income to cultivators. Efforts were made to induce a change in the traditional way of agriculture. Programmes for imparting training in agro and forest based industries were taken up so as to create opportunities of gainful employment. In many states Tribal Development Corporations were set up to play a key role in bringing about a new relationship between the tribal and the market economy through an integrated credit-cum-marketing service. The most backward groups among the tribal communities, many of them at pre-agricultural stage of economy, were identified and special programmes were taken for their development. The administrative structure in tribal areas was reviewed and restructured so as to provide effective services to the tribal people. The areas under the Fifth Schedule have been rationalised so as to provide a more effective protection to the tribals and for better implementation of plans.

For operational purposes the Tribal Sub-Plan areas have been organised into Integrated Tribal Development Projects (ITDPs). It is the level at which entire development efforts have been integrated. The problem of the areas, resource potentiality and felt needs of the people have been tackled under the programme implemented in these projects.

The programmes under the Tribal Sub-Plan are supported by the sectoral outlays in the State Plan, Central Programmes and institutional finance available for different programmes. Besides this *Special Central Assistance* is provided to the Tribal Sub-Plan to fill-in the gaps so as to make the delivery of services complete and to accelerate the programmes under State and Central Plans. In the Fifth Plan the quantum of outlay in the Tribal Sub-Plan was determined from out of the divisible part of state plan on the basis of (a) total population, (b) geographical area, (c) the relative development and (d) state of services in the sub-plan areas. Similarly, the Central Ministries were required to identify the programmes relating to tribal development concerning their sectors.

The outlays determined for tribal areas were made nondivertible. Therefore the States with large tribal population introduced separate budget heads under each major functional head. In other States the entire outlay on the Tribal Sub-Plan has been brought under a single demand.

While programmes of a local nature will be given attention at the ITDP level, the major thrust areas of the Tribal Sub-Plan of a State would be identified; these thrust areas could be different for the different regions of the country. Some of the major thrust areas such as shifting cultivation, horticulture, credit-cum-marketing, minor irrigation, forestry-oriented programme, programme for landless, pasture development, animal husbandry and education have been identified after a review of States' efforts in implementation of sub-plans. A clear perspective of these programmes will be prepared and other economic programmes will be built around them. Primitive communities will get special attention. In its report published in 1978 – the Union Home Ministry had defined the following criteria to identify a primitive tribe: (i) Primitive style of agriculture (ii) Illiteracy (iii) Sedentary or static groups. In the process of development the traditional craftsmen in the tribal areas have been particularly adversely affected because they are facing an unequal competition from the products of large scale industries. While the ITDPs had identified these groups, suitable programmes were yet to be concretised. In those regions where forests occupy a large area, balanced development of the tribal community and their economy based on development of forestry and allied activities was to be planned.

The Government of Maharashtra and the Integrated Area Development Approach

Realisation of the fact that, "all the planned activity undertaken for this section (Adivasis, Vimukta Jatis and Nomadic Tribes) uptil now lacked both the direction and integration in its format, design and implementation", and that "there were hardly few schemes which were designed to benefit this section directly", prompted the Maharashtra State Government to switch on to a new approach. The experience of the past four Five Year Plans made the Government to think that it was desirable to undertake the developmental activities for these communities through Integrated Area Development Programme. This approach would be 'practical' and would facilitate drawing up of a required design of a plan specially tailored for the needs of the tribal section of the population.

It was therefore decided by the State Government to undertake speedy steps for all-round development of the Adivasis through the approach which has come to be known as Integrated Area Development Approach, manifest in the Ashram-Shala (School) complex. It had the following salient features:

1. The Approach envisages selection of compact areas of about 5000 to 7000 population in scheduled areas and hilly areas to start multifarious developmental activities.
2. The Ashram-School Complex will be the focul centre, which would cover an approximate area of 7 miles of the above-mentioned compact area.
3. The speedy implementation of the all-sided welfare activities for the Adivasis' Socio-economic advancement in general and educational advancement in particular.
4. The complex activities would not conflict with the Block activities or other departmental activities.
5. The programme will be implemented in coordination with and technical guidance of the concerned Departments, such as Education Department; Buildings and Communications, Industries and Labour, Urban development, Public Health and Housing, Rural Development Department, Forest, Agriculture and Cooperation Department etc. under the direct control of Government through the agency of the Department of Tribal Welfare.

Each Ashram Shala Complex will be consisting of the following activities:

(i) Ashram School,
(ii) Hostel,
(iii) Balwadi,
(iv) Agriculture Demonstration Farm,
(v) Dairy Husbandry Unit,
(vi) Preventive Curative and Health Services Unit,
(vii) Pre-Vocational Training Centre.

The Tribal Sub-Plan in Maharashtra State

The key-note of the Sub-plan framed by the Government of Maharashtra is a 'unified command approach' with selective growth centres and viable melded instruments to take care of the economics of the tribal areas. The important tenets are:

1. Instead of operating only individually oriented schemes, all the schemes will be integrated with a view to develop an area i.e. an *Integrated Area Development Approach* (IADP Approach).
2. The on-going area development approach (Ashram Shala) schemes will be used as a focal point in and around which an extended network culminating in a Growth Centre will be operated.
   This Centre will make available to groups of villages, basic infrastructural facilities to release economic and environmental forces required for development.
3. A new institutionalised credit-cum-marketing Cooperative agency will be intermeshed at appropriate points with the aim of breaking the moneylender-cum-trader Complex by touching the total economic life of Adivasis.
4. Operating various development schemes in an integrated manner over a compact area within a given time span through an independent Tribal authority.
5. Restructuring of other on-going schemes like wells, provision of electricity, health facilities etc. to suit the needs of individuals and areas.

The important principles adopted for the sub-plan are briefly stated below:

(i) *The Principle of Non-Divertability*

Once a plan frame and resource mobilisation and allocation therefor is approved by the Cabinet and when for translation of this decision annual sectoral provisions are made in the Budget, irrespective of the sector under which funds have been provided for in the Budget for the specific purpose of the Tribal Sub-Plan, all such funds should be pooled under the special major head. The control over the special major head will rest with the high power authority in-charge of the deployment of Tribal Sub-Plan funds and consequently no diversion of these funds without active concurrence of the high power body will become feasible.

(ii) *The Principal of Non-lapsability*

In the event of partial non-absorption of funds estimated and approved for any given plan year and automatic credit to that extent will be given to that sector in the succeeding financial year's plan allocation. It hardly needs to be said that this procedure will be within the upper limit of the total sectoral allocation for the entire plan period. This device in practice will do away with the concept and constraints of some how managing to finish actual implementation of a given scheme and therefore consequential booking of expenditure (which leads to in more than one case of hurry and unimaginative haste of booking expenditure around 31st of March every year) by 31st March of that financial year. This will ensure that the pace of implementation of schemes can be more realistic and the actual booking of expenditure can be more purposive thus avoiding infructuous expenditure. It also ensures removal of the element of uncertainty in the matter of completion of schemes which remain incomplete at the end of a given financial year.

In pure budgetary theory, it really means a total commitment on the part of the State Government at the beginning of the Tribal Sub-Plan to an irrevocable decision (unforeseen situations, or an act of God including) regarding the gross size of resource deployment from the State Sector for the entire Sub-Plan period. This, in other words, means that once the State Government commits itself to a decision of the total size of State Sector's deployment for the entire Sub-Plan period, then, temporary ways and means constraints will not affect year to year allocation of funds Sub-Plan sector-wise and in turn for the gross deployment for the whole Sub-Plan itself over the entire Sub-Plan period.

(iii) *Excise Policy*

The Central Cabinet have approved of a broad strategy. Broadly, it means:

(a) So far as vend shops for manufactured liquor are concerned, all such vend shops in the Tribal areas will be closed;

(b) The restrictions of production of home brewed forms of liquor traditional to the tribal communities shall be totally removed, so far as tribals are concerned, and they may be allowed to freely produce such liquor and consume it which includes a local village distribution, but precludes inter-village sales;

(c) So far as tapping of toddy trees are concerned, the licences to tap toddy shall be issued only to the tribals in the Sub-Plan areas.

Wherever in a given particular village, a local elected representative by a formal resolution so requests, to the extent of that tribal village total prohibition will be introduced.

A Strategy for Primitive Tribes and Extremely Backward Tribal Groups

While conceding that the tribal communities as a whole are a way behind certain non-tribal communities in the pace of development, the Government of India in their guidelines have recognised that even amongst tribals there are isolated small groups who are extremely backward and even occasionally at primitive levels of either hunting and food gathering or in a very few cases at the level of Stone Age, i.e. at an extremely lower level of acculturation.

In the guidelines for the Tribal Sub-Plan, a recommendation has been made for devisement of special programmes for such particularly primitive group, if any, in a given State. The Government of India, in the Ministry of Home Affairs, have appointed a special technical group of anthropological experts to identify such groups of primitive tribals. Fortunately, a preponderant majority of tribals in Maharashtra are at a State of development far above the primitive level. The only group of tribals which has been so identified for this purpose, in Maharashtra, is that of Madia-Gonds, mainly in Chandrapur (now in Gadchiroli) District. Due to certain economic reasons, perhaps, we may include another small group of Katkaris in the thana and Kolaba districts.

It was stated in their policy perspective by the Maharashtra Government that "What needs to be done is to send out expert teams for making a special on-the-spot study to identify the immediate problems for these groups and when this is done, special programmes for these groups of people could be devised. It has been indicated by the Government of India that additive support from the

Government of India component for these programmes can be expected form the Central Government. It will suffice tentatively if we may make a gross ad hoc reservation of, say, 50 lakhs of rupees for such special programmes, as may be devised for these groups. This will be State sector additive for these people in the sense that benefits flowing from the general Tribal Sub-Plan frame will also be available to these special primitive groups of people also.

Growth Centres

From 1st April, 1975 the Government of India had stopped giving financial aid for the T.D. Blocks and the State Government had to make the necessary arrangements. It was decided to provide a focal point in between the taluka headquarters and Ashram School Complex. It was decided that for a group of six Ashram School Complexes or for 25,000 population, one Growth Centre will be created. Under one growth centre there would be two new agencies for dispensing credit and offering marketing facilities, one agency covering about 12,500 population and below such agency there would be three Ashram School Complexes each covering a population of about 3000. The immediate primary needs would be satisfied at the lowest point i.e. the Ashram School Complex, a bit more complicated and yet all embracing economic need viz. credit and marketing facility will be satisfied at the next higher point i.e. the Adivasi Cooperative Society level and lastly the remaining infrastructural arrangements would be available at the Growth Centre which will consist of the following:

(i) Demonstration farms,
(ii) Soil Testing Laboratory,
(iii) Bazar facility,
(iv) Forest, agro-based and other small scale industries complex,
(v) Multi-purpose vocational training workshop,
(vi) Primary health unit and rural hospital,
(vii) S.T. Bus Stop,
(viii) Community Recreation Centre,
(ix) Godown facilities,
(x) Inspection Huts,
(xi) Posts and Telegraphs Office,
(xii) Police Outpost,

(xiii) Water Supply and Electricity Unit,
(xiv) Growth Centre Office.

The Sub-Plan is proposed to be made applicable to:

(a) Talukas/Panchayat Samitis where the over-all population of adivasis exceeds 50 per cent.
(b) Such Talukas/Panchayat Samitis where the over all population of tribals may not exceed 50 per cent but the total number of villages in such an administrative unit having population of Adivasis in excess of 50 per cent predominates.
(c) Existing Tribal Blocks (including those already proposed to Government of India whether they are in the schedule areas or otherwise).
(d) Tribal areas not covered under the above categories but where it is proposed to start T.D. Blocks.

The Machinery for Implementation

Under the new sub-plan pattern which had commenced from the 14th August, 1975, the administrative organisation was initially headed by a Steering Committee at the State level with the Finance Minister as Chairman and Secretary to the Government in the Department of Social Welfare as its Member-Secretary. The Tribes Advisory Committee will advise the Steering Committee. Initially the Tribal Commissioner will be the Chief Administrator, later on there would be two authorities viz. one each for the Sahyadri region and the other for Gondwana region with headquarters at Nasik and Nagpur respectively.

Under the Tribal Commissioner, responsible to him would be a Deputy Commissioner (Tribal), and the Chief Executive Officers who will be designated as Deputy Commissioner (Tribal) would be responsible for the District. He would be of the rank of a collector. At the Growth Centre there would be an *Adivasi Vikas Adhikari* who will be the head at the Centre. The other departments would be coordinated from the Commissioner's level to the V.D.O.'s level as shown in the organisation chart.

Later there were some changes in the administrative set up and at present the administrative set up in Maharashtra is as follows:

The Administrative Set-up for the Tribal Sub-Plan
(w.e.f. 1st May, 1983)

Mantralaya Level	*Tribal Development Department*
	Secretary and Tribal Commissioner – (Head of the Department)
Division Level	Additional Tribal Commissioners at Nasik and Nagpur
District Level	Deputy Commissioner – Tribal — Collector of the District
	Addl. Deputy Commissioner — Chief Executive Officer of the Zilla Parishad
Project Level	Project Officer (Rank of Dy. Collector — Class I)
	Project Staff Pattern under P.O.

Post	Number
Assistant Project Officer	1
Research Assistant	1
Stenographer	1
Accountant/Head Clerk	1/1
Driver	1
Peon	1
Total	7

The Secretary and Tribal Commissioner who is the Head of the Department of Tribal Development, acts as a liaison between the Government of India the State Mantralaya and the State Legislature. He also coordinates the Development departments at the State level, and serves the Cabinet Sub-committee.

The State Level Cabinet Committee is headed by the Chief

Minister and decides the policy, proposals and matters related to the Tribal Sub-Plan.

There is a Special Executive Committee of the District Planning and Development Council. The In-charge Minister of the District (*Palakmantri*) is the Chairman and one of the Tribal MLA's is the Vice-Chairman, Deputy Tribal Commissioner i.e. Collector of the District is its Member-Secretary. While formulating the plans and programmes and while assessing the progress of Tribal Sub-Plan area all the concerned Heads of Departments are associated with the committee.

In recent years an Implementation Committee is formed at Project Level. The Additional Tribal Commissioner of the concerned division is Chairman and all implementing officers at the District Level similarly the officers at the Project and Tahsil Level are members of the Committee. Some representatives of local bodies and important institutions are also nominated as members. This Committee looks after the formulation and implementation of the Tribal Sub-Plan in the Project Area.

The Maharashtra State Tribal Development Corporation with its headquarters at Nasik is entrusted with the work of monopoly procurement of agricultural produce and minor forest produce in T.S.P. area. The Sub-Agents of the Corporation are the Adivasi Cooperative Societies functioning in the area.

The Director, Tribal Development with headquarters at Nasik is entrusted with the implementation of two important schemes viz.,

(i) Government Ashram Schools/Post-Basic Ashram Schools and the Hostels for Scheduled Tribes.

(ii) Supply of electric motor pumps and oil engines to Adivasi cultivators.

There are two Regional Deputy Directors (Nasik and Nagpur) for the implementation and Tribal Development Officers at the Regional/District Level.

The Coverage under Tribal Sub-Plan in Maharashtra

The criteria for selecting the area for T.S.P. have been adopted from the guidelines of the Government of India and include:

1. All scheduled areas
2. All Tribal Development Blocks
3. All Tahsils having 50 per cent or more concentration of tribal population.
4. Villages of areas which constitute Tribal 'pockets' in or around the above-mentioned areas or which are contagious and have a predominantly tribal population and as such the inclusion of which is administratively essential.

In the main Tribal Sub-Plan of the Government of Maharashtra 11 districts and 47 tahsils consisting of 5,122 villages are covered. The districts include — Thane, Nasik, Pune, Ahmadnagar, Dhule, Jalgaon, Amravati, Nanded, Yeotmal, Chandrapur and Gadchiroli.

The Maharashtra State Government has sponsored Additional Tribal Sub-Plan areas in four districts viz., Raigad, Nagpur, Bhandara and Chandrapur including 29 Tahsils and 1,038 villages covered.

Under the Modified Area Development Approach 18 pockets with Tribal concentrations have been selected spreadover 596 villages covered.

Thus under all the above categories the T.S.P. coverage spreads over —

Districts	:	15
Tahsils	:	75
Villages	:	6,756
Towns	:	14

As per 1981 Census figures the total Tribal population of Maharashtra is 57.72 Lakhs i.e. 9.20 per cent of total population of the State.

The population covered under T.S.P. is 25.70 Lakhs i.e. 44.53 per cent of the total tribal population.

Additional Coverage

By the end of the Seventh Five Year Plan the scheduled tribes population was hundred per cent covered under the Tribal Sub-Plan, as, apart from the I.T.D.P.s, the M.A.D.A. (Modified Area Development) pockets, clusters and primitive tribal groups, and even the dispersed tribals were being assisted through special Central Assistance. Although, Tribal Sub-Plan is a Plan within the State Plan, it is more than a Plan in the sense that certain regulatory functions such as preparation of land records, repair and maintenance of tanks and other assets were a part of the Tribal Sub-Plan strategy.

Tribal Sub-plan Coverage in Maharashtra at a Glance

TABLE 3.1: Districtwise Total and Tribal Population of Maharashtra State

(as per 1981 census)

Sl. No.	State/District	Population as per 1981 Census		Percentage of Tribal Population with Total Population
		Total	Tribal	
1	2	3	4	5
	Maharashtra State	627.84	57.72	9.19
	Nagpur Division			
26	Wardha	9.27	1.42	15.35
27	Nagpur	25.89	3.53	13.65
28	Bhandara	18.38	2.98	16.22
29	Chandrapur	14.18	2.99	21.07
30	Gadchiroli	6.37	2.51	39.32

TABLE 3.2: S.T. Population in Maharashtra in Three Decades

Sl. No.	Population	1981	1971	1961
1.	Total Population (in Lakhs)	627.84	504.12	395.54
2.	Tribal Population (in Lakhs)	57.72	29.54	23.07
3.	Percentage of Tribal Population to Total Population	9.19	5.86	5.83

TABLE 3.3: Tribal Sub-Plan Area — Important Indicators of Maharashtra State

Sl. No.	Items	Particulars (Population in Lakhs)
1.	Total Tribal population (1981 Census)	57.72
2.	Total population covered under Tribal Sub-plan (Scheduled Areas + A.T.S.P. + M.A.D.A. + Mini-MADA, 4 Pockets)	48.20
3.	Tribal population covered under T.S.P.	27.58
4.	Tribal Population outside T.S.P. Area	30.14
5.	Percentage of Tribal Population covered under T.S.P. to the States total S.T. Population	47.78
6.	Percentage of Tribal Population outside the sub-plan area and States total population	52.28
7.	No. of Districts covered under T.S.P.	18
8.	No. of Tahsils fully covered under T.S.P.	81
9.	No. of Tahsils not fully covered under T.S.P.	20
10.	Total No. of Tahsils covered	101
11.	No. of Integrated Tribal Development Projects (I.T.D.P.s)	19
12.	No. of Special I.T.D.P. Project for Primitive Tribes (at Bhamragad)	1
13.	No. of Towns covered	13

TABLE 3.4: Districtwise Tribal Population in Tribal Sub-plan Area (T.S.P. area) and Outside Tribal Sub-Plan Area (O.T.S.P. area) as per 1981 Census

Sl. No.	State/District	Scheduled Tribe Population (per 1981 census)					
		In Tribal Sub-plan area (T.S.P.)			Outside Tribal Sub-Plan area		
		Tribal population	Percentage with		Tribal population	Percentage with	
			States 57.72 Lakhs Total Tribal Population	States 27.58 Lakhs Total Tribal Population		District Total Tribal Population	States Tribal Population 36.14 Lakhs O.T.S.P. area
1	2	3	4	5	6	7	8
	Maharashtra State	27.58	47.78	100.00	30.14	52.22	100.00
Nagpur Division							
26	Wardha	0.11	0.19	0.39	1.31	92.25	4.35
27	Nagpur	0.39	0.68	1.41	3.14	88.95	10.42
28	Bhandara	1.00	1.73	3.63	1.98	66.44	6.57
29	Chandrapur	1.36	2.36	4.93	1.63	54.52	5.41
30	Gadchiroli	2.25	3.90	8.16	0.26	10.36	0.86
Nagpur Division Total		5.11	8.85	18.53	8.33	62.03	27.64

TABLE 3.5: Total Number of Ashram Schools and Post-Basic Ashram-Schools in T.S.P. and O.T.S.P. area at the end of 1986-87

Sl. No.	Particular	No. of Ashram Schools			No. of Post Basic Ashram Schools		
		T.S.P.	O.T.S.P.	Total	T.S.P.	O.T.S.P.	Total
1	2	3	4	5	6	7	8
1.	Government	262	68	330	84	17	101
2.	Voluntary Agencies	79	18	97	32	10	42
	Total	341	86	427	116	27	143

TABLE 3.6: I.T.D.P.-wise Number of Villages/Towns/M.A.D.A. Pockets, (under Scheduled Area)/Mini M.A.D.A. pockets and A.T.S.P. areas of Maharashtra State

Sl. No.	District	Name of I.T.D.P.	No. of Villages included as per 1971 Census				Total No. of villages
			Schedul-ed area	M.A.D.A. pocket	Mini-M.A.D.A. pocket	A.T.S.P. area	
1	2	3	4	5	6	7	8
State Total		19	5365 (13)	1055	188	816	7424 (13)
18	Gadchiroli	Etapalli-18	650	—	—	—	650
		Dhanora-19	752	—	—	44	796
District-wise Total			1402	—	—	44	1446

There is one separate project at Bhamragad, District Gadchiroli for primitive tribes.

TABLE 3.7: Number of Villages covered under Scheduled Area (Tahsilwise)/M.A.D.A. Pocket/Mini-M.A.D.A. Pocket/A.T.S.P. Area of Maharashtra State (1971 Census)

Sl. No.	District	Tahsil	No. of Villages/Towns under						Total Col. 4+7+8+9
			Scheduled area T.S.P. (Main) area, T.S.P. area	M.A.D.A. Pocket			Mini-M.A.D.A. Pockets (14) Mini-M.A.D.A Pockets	A.T.S.P. area	
				Old (17)	New (13)	Total (30) M.A.D.A Pockets			
1	2	3	4	5	6	7	8	9	10
Maharashtra State		Total	5365 (13)	585	470	1055	188	816	7424 (13)
17	Gadchiroli	91 Sironcha*	124	—	—	—	—	—	124
		92 Aheri*	214	—	—	—	—	—	214
		93 Etapalli*	312	—	—	—	—	—	312
		94 Gadchiroli	62	—	—	—	—	1	63
		95 Armori	74	—	—	—	—	2	76
		96 Chamorshi	132	—	—	—	—	41	173
		97 Kurkheda*	212	—	—	—	—	—	212
		98 Dhanora*	272	—	—	—	—	—	272
	District	Total	1402	—	—	—	—	44	1446

* Tahsil covered fully under T.S.P. area.

TABLE 3.8: I.T.D.P.-wise Scheduled Tribe Population covered under T.S.P./M.A.D.A., Pockets/Mini-M.A.D.A. Pockets/and A.T.S.P. areas of Maharashtra State as per 1981 Census

Sl. No.	District	Name of the I.T.D.P.	(1) Provisional, (2) Population in Lakhs				
			No. of Villages (Urban areas) covered as per 1971 census	Population covered 1981		Percentage of S.T. population covered in T.S.P. area with	
				Total	Tribal	Total S.T. population in T.S.P. area of the state i.e. (27.58 Lakhs)	Total S.T. population (57.72 Lakhs)
1	2	3	4	5	6	7	8
	State Total		7424 (13)	48.42	27.58	100.00	47.48
14	Gadchiroli	17 Etapalli	650	1.79	0.95	3.45	1.65
		18 Dhanora	796	2.62	1.30	4.71	2.25
	District Total		1446	4.41	2.25	8.16	3.90

TABLE 3.9: Number of Villages, Total and Tribal Population covered under M.A.D.A. Pockets as per 1981 Census in Maharashtra position as on 1-4-1987 (Provisional)

Sl. No.	District	Names of M.A.D.A. pockets	No. of Villages	Population (1981)		Tribal Concentration	Major Tribals residing
				Total	Tribal		
1	2	3	4	5	6	7	8
	State Total	30	1,055	4,66,174	2,67,867	57.46	
11	Chandrapur	28 Sindewahi 29 Nagbhid	54 43	23.698 17.231	12.995 6.110	54.84 53.97	Gond, Kolam, Pardhan

TABLE 3.10: Total No. of Scheduled Tribe Families and those below poverty line in the Sub-plan Area of Maharashtra State

Sl. No.	I.T.D.P.	S.T. Families		Percentage of Col. No. 4 to Col. No. 3
		Total	Below Poverty Line	
1	2	3	4	5
16	Gadchiroli (Etapalli)	14,918	14,508	97.25
17	Gadchiroli (Dhanora)	21,377	14,884	69.62
	State Total	4,35,258	3,95,647	90.89

Source: Universal Bench Mark Survey, 1980.

TABLE 3.11: District-wise Scheduled Tribe Families below Poverty Line (as per D.R.D.A. Survey, 1980)

Sl. No.	District	Scheduled Tribe Families	
		Total (Rural)	Below Poverty Line
1	2	3	4
28	Gadchiroli	1,01,832	59,440
29	Chandrapur		
	Total for the State	9,79,817	6,24,521

TABLE 3.12: Total number of Scheduled Tribe families, landless Scheduled Tribe families with their percentages with total in Tribal Sub-Plan area of Maharashtra State

Sl. No.	State/Region District/I.T.D.P.	Total Scheduled Tribe families (B.M.S.)	Landless Families		Percentage of total
			Total (S.C./S.T., and others)	Tribal	
1	2	3	4	5	6
	Maharashtra State (Sub-plan Area)	4,35,258	3,08,281	1,93,212	70.88
13	Gadchiroli District	36,295	26,057	11,095	42.58
	(a) Ettapalli I.T.D.P.	14,918	13,172	5,086	38.61
	(b) Dhanora I.T.D.P.	21,377	12,885	6,009	46.63
14	Chandrapur District	17,405	21,425	6,354	29.33
	(a) Rajura I.T.D.P.	5,954	7,001	2,422	34.60
	(b) Chimur I.T.D.P.	11,451	14,424	3,932	27.26

Source: Bench Mark Survey, 1980.

TABLE 3.13: Forest Areas in Maharashtra State (1980)*

(*Area in Sq. Km*)

Sl. No.	District	Geographical area of District	Forest area of District	Percentage of forest area to total geographical area
1	2	3	4	5
Total	Maharashtra State	3,07,762	64,224,19	20.87
VI	*Nagpur Division*			
1.	Wardha	6,307	885,89	14.05
2.	Nagpur	9,928	2,752,53	27.72
3.	Bhandara	9,214	4,560,67	49.50
4.	Chandrapur	25,641	18,492,71	72.12
	Total	51,090	26,691,80	52.24

Source: Forest Department, Pune.

TABLE 3.14: Area Under Different Categories of Forest in Tribal Sub-Plan of Maharashtra State

(*Area in Hectares*)

Sl. No.	State/Region/ District I.T.D.P.	Total Geographical area	Area under different categories of forest			Percentage of total forest area to total Geographical area
			Protected	Reserved	Total	
1	2	3	4	5	6	7
	Maharashtra State	48,53,560	7,16,118	15,78,830	22,94,948	47.28
13	Gadchiroli District	10,80,229	6,07,004	1,36,596	7,43,600	68.84
	(a) Ettapalli I.T.D.P.	7,90,615	6,07,004	30,886	6,37,890	80.69
	(b) Dhanora I.T.D.P.	2,89,614	—	1,05,710	1,05,710	36.50

Source: Bench Mark Survey, 1980.

TABLE 3.15: District-wise Primary Schools and Enrolment in Tribal Sub-Plan Area

Sl. No.	District	Total No. of Institutions	Total Enrolment	Total Teachers	Trained Teachers	Percentage of Trained Teachers
1	2	3	4	5	6	7
13	Chandrapur	502	49,902	1,242	1,115	89.8
14	Gadchiroli	622	47,160	1,150	779	67.7
Total	Gondwana Region	2,337	2,18,361	5,270	4,394	83.4
Total	Maharashtra State T.S.P.	6,606	6,00,710	16,040	13,625	84.9

TABLE 3.16: District-wise Number of Villages and Towns covered in M.A.D.A. Pockets, Mini-M.A.D.A. Pockets and A.T.S.P. area of Maharashtra State as on 1-4-1987

Sl. No.	District	No. of I.T.D.P.	No. of villages (towns) included in				Total No. of Villages (Towns)
			Scheduled area	K.M.A.D.A. Pockets	Mini-M.A.D.A. Pockets	A.T.S.P. Area	
1	2	3	4	5	6	7	8
	Maharashtra State-18		5,365 (13)	1,055	188	816	7,424 (13)
16	Chandrapur	2	182	97	—	465	744
17	Gadchiroli	2	1,402	—	—	44	1,446

4

IMPLEMENTATION OF SCHEMES

Before knowing the various schemes under the tribal development programme we must know the various agencies entrusted with the implementation of these schemes. As our pattern emphasises the role of the State in bringing about welfare and development of the weaker section the burden of implementation was mainly on the Government Departments and other bodies like Corporations, Cooperative Societies etc. formed by the Government and functioning under their control. Voluntary organisations were not given any important role in this pattern.

To start with, we shall acquaint ourselves with the agencies/departments implementing the schemes, then the schemes proper and later with the specific schemes implemented by the departments in the area under study.

The Implementing Agencies/Different Departments

The Tribal Development Department was established at the Secretariat *Mantralaya* level in 1983 and a separate Directorate for Tribal Development was established with headquarters at Nasik. Offices of Tribal Development Officers under this Directorate were established at (1) Thane, (2) Nasik, (3) Pune, (4) Jalgaon, (5) Nanded, (6) Chandrapur, (7) Yavatmal, (8) Amravati, (9) Nagpur. (10) Nandurbar (Dist. Dhule), (11) Dahanu (Distt. Thane), (12) Shahapur (Distt. Thane), (13) Kalvan (Distt. Nasik), (14) Rajur (Distt. Ahmednagar), (15) Gondia (Distt. Bhandara), (16) Aheri (Distt. Gadchiroli), (17) Talodi (Distt. Dhule), (18) Gadchiroli, (19) Aurangabad and (20) Bombay City (at Goregaon).

The different schemes implemented through this department include:

(i) Ashram Schools (Government Ashram Schools)
(ii) Government Hostels for Tribal Students (*Shasakiya Vastigriha*).
(iii) Grant-in-aid Ashram Schools and Post-Basic Ashram Schools run by Voluntary organisation.
(iv) Supply of electric motor-pumps to tribal farmers through T.D.O.).
(v) Supply of oil-engines to tribal farmers (through T.D.O.).

The Maharashtra State Co-operative Tribal Development (M.S.C.T.D.) Corporation

Established in 1972 it operates in Pune, Ahmadnagar, Nasik, Thane, Raigad, Dhule, Jalgaon, Nagpur, Amravati, Yavatmal, Bhandara, Gadchiroli, Chandrapur and Nanded district and in 75 talukas from these districts.

The Adivasi Co-operative Societies (A.C.Ss.) were established to fill-in the vacuum created due to the abolition of private money-lenders, traders from tribal areas. So far, 258 A.C.Ss. were established, which work in coordination with the Corporation for their sale and purchase transactions.

The Schemes run by the M.S.C.T.D. Corporation include:

(i) Monopoly Grain Purchase Scheme
(ii) Grain purchase through the A.C.Ss.
(iii) Purchase of Minor Forest Produce (like Myrobalan, *Chironjee*, Gum, *Mahua* flowers, *Mahua* seeds etc.)
(iv) Distribution of Consumption Loans (*Khavti* loans) to tribal families.
(v) Supply of food-grains, other material of Ashram Schools, Hostels etc.

Schemes operated through the Agriculture Department

These schemes are operated either through the Zilla Parishad/ Panchayat Samiti or through the department directly:

(i) Crop-protection (Farm in-put kits are provided)
(ii) Grants (50% basis) for purchase of bullock-carts or pairs of bullocks for farming or for transport business.

(iii) Soil-testing (once in three years through the Agriculture Department).
(iv) *Soil Conservation Scheme.
(v) **Aayakut* Scheme (proper distribution of water from minor irrigation projects).

Other schemes operated through the Agriculture Department include:

(i) Installation of gobar-gas plants.
(ii) Encouraging production of pulses.
(iii) Encouraging tribal farmers to take two crops.
(iv) Organising educational tours of tribal farmers.
(v) Supply of instruments for crop protections.
(vi) Demonstration plots of oil-seeds (specially in MADA pockets).
(vii) Training of tribal boys in the repairs of agricultural implements and in agriculture.

The Horticulture Department's Schemes

Operated through the District Horticulture Officer, those include:

(i) Nursery
(ii) Grafting of fruit trees.
(iii) Grants and training for horticultural development.
(iv) Kitchen gardens and courtyard garden (*Gharkul*).
(v) Vegetable gardens.
(vi) Crop-protection schemes.

The State Education Department

The different schemes implemented through this department include:

(i) Creches, balwadis, primary and middle schools.
(ii) Book-bank scheme for tribal students.

---

* Both these schemes operated through the Soil Conservation Officers.

(iii) Construction of Primary-School building.
(iv) Grants to Zilla Parishads for construction of houses for Primary School Teachers.
(v) Special facilities to tribal students in Primary Schools.
(vi) Middle schools.
(vii) Grant-in-aid to schools run by voluntary organisations.
(viii) Adult Education Programmes (through the Directorate of Adult Education).
(ix) Teachers' Training and Training of Adult Education Functionaries.
(x) Scholarships and freeships to tribal students.
(xi) School Complex Scheme/Residential School Schemes.
(xii) Prizes to Primary School Teachers from tribal areas (an incentive scheme).

The Fisheries Department: It organises training with stipend and supplies fish-seed, instruments for catching fishes, loans for construction or repairs to tanks, fishing boats etc. Nylon nets and fish-seed are specially provided to the Madia tribals from Bhamragad (Distt. Gadchiroli) free of cost.

The Animal Husbandry Department: It distributes milch cattle, bulls, goats, hens and chickens (Rhode-island red type), pigs and fodder. Special training in cattle farming etc. is also provided to tribal youths.

The Dairy Department has schemes for rearing-up of cows and buffaloes, training in milk preservation techniques, fodder development etc.

The Public Health Departments establishes and runs Rural Hospitals, Primary Health Centres, Mobile Health-care Units, Preventive measures including inoculations, medical check-up and treatment to tribal children in schools and hostels, mothers' care and child care programmes and the family welfare programmes. Para-medical personnel are also trained for the purpose.

Under the *Rural Development Schemes* are covered digging of wells, tube-wells, nutrition to children in schools, nutrition to pregnant and nursing mothers and special Applied Nutrition Programmes.

The Social Welfare Department gives free concessions and scholarships/freeships to tribal students in schools/colleges etc. Grants are given to hostels run for tribal students by voluntary organisations. Grants are also given to creches and balwadis.

The Forest Department provides bamboo, grass, firewood etc. to tribals, gives protection to tribal agriculture and other occupations as per laws. Labour work is also provided in forest operations. Forest Labour Cooperative Societies have been established whose collaboration is obtained in the felling of trees etc. by the department.

A few schemes like supply of implements/tools for earth work, supply of bullock-carts were also taken-up in addition to usual functions.

The Industries Department, the Employment Department etc. have various self-employment schemes etc. for tribal youths. Training as well as credit facilities are made available.

The Land Development Banks and the *Nationalised Banks* have various schemes with 50-75 per cent loan facilities with loan duration ranging between 7 to 10 years. These include loans for irrigation, land development, purchase of agricultural implements, bullocks and bullock-carts, crop-loans, supplementary occupations like dairy-farming, poultry, piggery, fishery, gobar-gas plants etc.

The Public Works Department constructs roads, bridges, cross-water drainage, Samaj-Mandirs (community halls), Schools building and maintains roads. It also provides employment to tribals on public works. Many Employment Guarantee Schemes are operated by the P.W.D. on its works.

Two special components for the T.S.P. area under special provisions are also available viz. Nucleus Budget Schemes and Special Central Assistance (S.C.A.) Schemes.

Different Schemes, Agencies and Expenditure Incurred

(Information Taken from the Office Records of Project Officer)

Different Schemes Implemented in the I.T.D.P. (Primitive Tribes) Specially for Bhamragad, Area

(Between 1981-82 up to 1986-87)

(I) *From Nucleus Budget*

(1) Scheme for development of land for cultivation.
(2) Scheme for supply of agricultural implements.

(3) Scheme for supply of seeds and fertilisers.
(4) Scheme for demonstration plots in the fields.
(5) Scheme for supply of bullocks.
(6) Scheme for concentrate of *Kadba-Kuti* (fodder) to bullocks.
(7) Scheme for establishment of pig units.
(8) Scheme for supply of mineral mixture, tonic powder to tribals' animals.
(9) Scheme for establishment of goat-unit.
(10) Scheme for plantation of fruit trees.
(11) Scheme for financial assistance to *Ghotuls* (Repairs/ Construction).
(12) Scheme for organisation of tribal dances.
(13) Scheme for providing financial assistance for improvement of tribal colony.
(14) Scheme for construction of *Bodis*.
(15) Scheme for supply of tools for land improvement.
(16) Scheme for supply of clothes.
(17) Scheme for supply of utensils to primitive Madias.
(18) Scheme for supply of pairs of bullocks and carts.
(19) Scheme for supply of concentrate for bullock pairs.
(20) Scheme for supply of B-Concentrate for bullock pairs.
(21) Scheme for appointment of tribal organisers on honorarium.
(22) Scheme for supply of agricultural inputs
(on 100% subsidy).
(Seed: Paddy-20 kg, Mixed manure: 50 kg, Urea: 50 kg, Copper auxichloride: 500 g, Fosmomadan: 250 ml).
(23) Scheme for establishment of housing colony for primitive tribals.
(24) Scheme for construction/completion of *Ghotuls*.
(25) Scheme for training of tribals in traditional metal craft.
(26) Scheme for training of tribals in traditional wood craft.
(27) Scheme for supply of uniforms to tribal students from schools/Anganwadis.
(28) Scheme for purchase of ferry boats.
(29) Scheme for supply of Mangalore tiles for roofing.
(30) Scheme for carpets and petromax to *Ghotuls*.
(31) Scheme for primary education to Madia boys.
(32) Scheme for aiding tribal patients during emergency.
(33) Scheme for supply of dress and other accessories to tribal dancing troupes.

(34) Scheme for ploughing of land of tribals by tractor (free).
(35) Scheme for levelling of land in tribals' farms/village.
(36) Scheme for organisation of community marriage of Madia tribals.
(37) Scheme for repairs to huts.
(38) Scheme for supply of hospital equipment to the Lok-Biradari Prakalpa (a private trusts' hospital) at Hemalkasa.
(39) Scheme for supply of school uniforms to tribal students at Lok-Biradari Prakalpa (L.B.P.), Hemalkasa.
(40) Scheme for supply of school equipment to L.B.P., Hemalkasa.
(41) Scheme for supply of medicines to L.B.P. Hospital, Hemalkasa.
(42) Scheme for supply of milk-cans/cycles for selling milk (2/3rd subsidy basis).
(43) Scheme for supply of utensils as gifts for undergoing family planning operation.
(44) Scheme for recruitment in employment.
(45) Scheme for subsidy for starting fair-price shop.
(46) Scheme for incentive to Madia parents for sending children to primary schools.
(47) Scheme for financial assistance to Madia youths for self employment.

(II) *From Special Central Assistance*

(Between 1981-82 to 86-87)

(1) Scheme for construction of community halls/centres — 'Samaj Mandirs'.
(2) Scheme for construction of huts with roofing tiles for Madias (on 100% subsidy).
(3) Scheme for free supply of agricultural in-puts, fertilizers, seeds etc. to Madia-Gond farmers.
(4) Scheme for supply of duster and sprayers to Madia cultivators.
(5) Scheme for land development for cultivation purposes.
(6) Scheme for supply of pairs of bullocks and bullocks-carts.
(7) Scheme for supply of goat unit.
(8) Scheme for supply of poultry birds (100% subsidy).
(9) Scheme for supply of Mangalore tiles for replacement of thatched roof.

(10) Scheme for supply of coarse woolen blankets (cumble) and coarse carpets to Madia-Gond families.
(11) Scheme for organisation of motivation camp.
(12) Scheme for study tour of Madias — trip to places.
(13) Scheme for purchase of jeep trolley.
(14) Scheme for construction of C.D. (Cross Drainage) works.
(15) Scheme for construction of staff quarters buildings/project complex (at Bhamragad).
(16) Scheme for construction of huts for Madias.
(17) Scheme for supply of writing material/uniforms to school-going students.
(18) Scheme for supply of oil engines.
(19) Scheme for supply of vegetable seed.
(20) Scheme for holding of training camp.
(21) Scheme for purchase of tractor-trolley.
(22) Scheme for supply of breeding bulls.
(23) Scheme for supply of pigs.
(24) Scheme for construction of huts-cum-shelter.
(25) Scheme for fish-farming in impoured water.
(26) Scheme for supply of writing material or dresses to tribal students.
(27) Scheme for establishment of Animal Husbandry Project at Bhamragad.
(28) Scheme for Training to tribal boys in animal husbandry and dairy work, and supply of one cow, calf etc.
(29) Scheme for supply of fish-seed and employees salary.

(III) *Other Schemes*

The Maharashtra State Tribal Development Corporation, through its sub-regional office at Aheri granted advances to the tribals for:

(i) Cycle-hire (Taxi) shop/cycle stores.
(ii) Grocery-shop/General Stores.
(iii) Vegetable shop
(iv) Brick-making.
(v) Broom-making and selling.
(vi) Sewing-machines.
(vii) Bullock-pairs and bullock-carts.
(viii) Carpentry

(ix) Goat-keeping
(x) Fishery
(xi) Poultry.

(2) Forest Department through the Divisional Forest Officers, Allapalli, implemented the following schemes:

(i) Supply of bullocks and bullock-carts.
(ii) Supply of *'Prakashtha Upakarans'*, i.e. Iron pan, pick-axe, spade and crow-bar to tribals (actually they are earth work implements).
(iii) Supply of bicycles to tribals.

(3) Directorate of Animal Husbandry, through their Deputy Director at Gadchiroli implemented the following schemes:

(i) Establishment of Animal Husbandry Training Centre at Bhamragad.
(ii) Training to Madia-Gond tribals from the Bhamragad area in Animal Husbandry and distribution of cows, goats, sheep etc.
(iii) Training in poultry to Madia women.
(iv) distribution of grants/loans for purchase of cows, goats pigs etc.

(4) The Directorate of Tribal Development through the Tribal Development Officer, Aheri implemented the following schemes:

(i) Starting and running Ashram School Complex.
(ii) Supply of oil engines (on 100% subsidy).
(iii) Supply of electric pumps (on 100% subsidy)
(iv) Starting and running Hostels for tribals students.
(v) Grants to Hostels run by voluntary organisations.
(vi) Scholarships to tribal students.

(5) Panchayat Samiti: The Project-cum-Block Development Officer implements the following schemes:

(i) Construction of gobar-gas/bio-gas plants.
(ii) Supply of agricultural inputs viz. seeds (Paddy), mixed

manures, urea, copper auxichloride, (C.O.C.) and fosmomadan to tribal farmers.

(6) *Public Works Department*

(i) Construction of roads, bridges.
(ii) Construction of small bridges/*ruptas*.
(iii) Construction of cross-drainage.
(iv) Construction of Community centres (Samaj Mandirs).
(v) Construction of Project office complex at Bhamragad.
(vi) Construction of Rest Houses/Office Buildings and Quarters.

All other schemes specially prepared under Nucleus Budget or Special Central Assistance, which could not be implemented through any particular development/service department were implemented by the Project Officer I.T.D.P. whose headquarters are at Bhamragad.

The coordination and monitoring of the different schemes noted above was also done by the Project Office, may be on paper only.

Special Schemes

Nucleus Budget Schemes

In order to encourage innovative schemes and to facilitate evoluation of schemes, tailor-made for solving problems of local importance the Government of Maharashtra created a special fund during 1981-82, called the Nucleus Budget. As per their Circular letter dated 14-10-1981 the Government kept this fund at the disposal of the Project Officers of the I.T.D.Ps. in order to enable them to carve out schemes of local applicability which are not included under the T.S.P. of that district. An elaborate procedure is not essential. The Maharashtra Tribal Development Corporation has, through this scheme given individual loans (50% interest-free loan and 50% subsidy) and an amount up to maximum Rs. 5,000 is sanctioned for skilled artisans to start, Maneri shop, grocery shops, vegetable shops, bamboo craft etc. to those who are below poverty line. In the primitive tribe area almost all are covered.

Special Central Assistance

The area being extremely backward and primitive, this assistance is specially given by the Centre for implementing schemes of local importance over and above the usual T.S.P. funds. Many innovative schemes can be taken-up under this assistance in the I.T.D.P.

Participation of other subject-matter departments in the area include the following:

Public Health

The Primary Health Centres (P.H.Cs.) at Etapalli and Bhamragad cater to the health needs of the tribals (to 64, and 159 villages respectively) in the area. Previously, due to faith in magic cure, supernatural powers and herbal medicines adopted by their *Bhagats/Permas* etc. they did not believe in medicines. But since last decade they are believing in medicines and there is very good response in the Lok-Biradari Hospital at Hemalkasa and the P.H.C. at Bhamragad. However it is now the Government which is lagging behind. Either there is no doctor at these centres or no medicines. The I.C.D.S. scheme has a provision of one medical officer. Since long the post is vacant and the medical officer at the P.H.C. is looking after both the jobs. It is high time that young, dedicated and qualified doctors should be appointed with full equipment and medicines.

Agriculture and Animal Husbandry

The State Departments of Agriculture and Animal Husbandry operates through Zilla Prishad and Panchayat Samiti. The Animal Husbandry Department is also having their Deputy Director at Gadchiroli who operates the Training and other relevant schemes at Bhamragad. The agricultural inputs to farmers are provided by, the Panchayat Samiti.

Education

The Education Department also operates through the Zilla Parishad and Panchayat Samiti. The primary schools and Middle/High schools are run by the Zilla Parishad. The Ashram Schools are under the supervision and control of the Tribal Development Officer.

The Panchayat Samiti

It operates the schemes related to Gobar-gas/Bio-gas, agricultural inputs, soil conservation schemes and other relevant schemes in Education, etc. However, the impact of their schemes has been more in the Etapalli I.T.D.P. than in the Bhamragad I.T.D.P. area. As discussed elsewhere in this report, they are unable to reach the inputs/services in time and as such their schemes don't reach the tribals. The gobar-gas scheme which is implemented on a large scale in the Etapalli area is a failure and people are persuaded to take it but are reluctant looking to the experience of others. The post of the Project-cum-Block Development Officer has remained vacant for many months and the staff position is also never up to date. They don't have suitable conveyance to communicate in the area, through all seasons. In fact the schemes of agricultural inputs, ploughing of land, irrigation, animal husbandry and Gobar-gas are the schemes which are very useful to tribals and can improve their lot. But they are not properly implemented.

Public Works

Roads and communication facilities should be given priority and developed within a definite span of time on 'war-footing'. Work once done must last long. Improvisation should be done away with. If need be, engineers from Army should be entrusted with the work and all mechanised support like bulldozers etc. be given. If there is all season communication between Etapalli to Bhamragad (Via Burgi-Kandodi) and between Bhamragad to Kuvvakodi and to Jagdalpur from above the hills with bridges on all rivers and rivulets. S.T. Buses can run in the area. This will accelerate process of development as development follows communication. In the second stage branching roads from these two trunk routes should be taken-up. Much waste of time, energy and material will be saved if this is done on top priority. Those engineers who will accept the challenge of showing results should specially be posted in the area.

Expenditure incurred on different schemes between 1981-82 to 1985-86 in shown in the tables that follow. Provision for 1986-87 scheme-wise are also given. (Figures taken from P.O.'s. office records).

I.T.D.P. Gadchiroli No. 1 Bhamragad Maharashtra

TABLE 4.1: Statement of Schemes taken as for the Benefit of Primitive Bada Madia Tribe of Bhamragad under *Nucleus Budget* for the Year 1981-82.

Sl. No.	Name of the Scheme	No. of Benefici-aries	No. of Villages	Expenditure Amount	Remarks
1	2	3	4	5	6
1.	Scheme for development of land cultivation	17	1	25,500.00	Binagunda, Turremarka
2.	Scheme for supply of Agricultural implements.	17	1	11,113.30	Fodewada, Damanmarka Kuwakodi, Pungasur
3.	Scheme for supply of seed, fertilizer etc.	17	1	24,848.00	
4.	Scheme for demonstration plot in the field of Madia-Gond	17	1	8,227.23	
5.	Scheme for supply of Bullocks	13	1	22,668.70	
6.	Scheme for supply of concentrate of Kadba — Kuti to bullocks	10	1	11,420.00	
7.	Scheme for establishment of pig unit.	18	1	24,000.00	
8.	Scheme for supply of minerals mixture, Tonic powder to animals of tribals	21	3	23,056.60	
9.	Scheme for establishment of goat unit.	12	1	24,000.00	

Contd.

TABLE 4.1 *Contd.*

1	2	3	4	5	6
10.	Scheme for plantation of fruit trees — Fodewada	—	1	31,802.00	
11.	do — Permalbhatti	—	1		
12.	do — Turremarka	—	1		
13.	do — Kuwakodi	—	1		
14.	Scheme for financial Assistance to Ghotul	5	5	15,421.50	
15.	Scheme for organization of Tribal Dances.	10	10	20,150.00	
16.	Schemes for providing financial Assistance for improvement of housing colony	17	1	20,150.00	
17.	Scheme for supply of constructions of *Bodis*	—	—	3,000.00	
18.	Scheme for supply of implements, tools for land improvement	94	8	25,000.00	
19.	Scheme for supply of clothes	90	8	50,000.00	
20.	Scheme for supply of utensils to primitive Madias.	90	8	45,000.00	
21.	Scheme for supply of bullock pairs	10	2	25,000.00	
22.	Scheme for supply of *concentrate* for bullock pairs	6	1	6,000.00	
23.	Scheme for supply of Bullock pairs	6	1	20,000.00	
24.	Scheme for supply of B-concentrate for bullock pairs	15	1	10,000.00	
25.	Scheme for supply of Appointment of Tribal Organizer on honorarium	4	4	19,405.75	
			Total Rs.	4,49,337.93	

I.T.D.P. Gadchiroli No. I Bhamragad, Maharashtra

TABLE 4.2: Expenditure Under Nucleus Budget for the Year 1982-83

Sl. No.	Name of the Scheme	No. of Beneficiaries	No. of Villages	Expenditure Amount	Remarks
1.	Scheme for supply of (free) inputs	32	10	11,430	
2.	Scheme for supply of goat unit	25	7	25,000	
3.	Scheme for supply of pig unit	20	4	25,000	
4.	Scheme for Establishment of housing colony for 10 families of Binagunda	10	1	20,000	
5.	Scheme for provision of fund for completion of 5 *Ghotuls*	—	5		
6.	Scheme for fruit plantation	—	—		
7.	Scheme for training of tribals in traditional metal craft.	11	1	8,410	
8.	Scheme for training of tribals in traditional wood craft.	11	1	8,660	
9.	Scheme for supply uniforms to Adiwasi students of Ashram-Lok Biradari Prakalpa, Hemalkasa	216	1	25,000	A.S., Hemalkasa, LBP
10.	Scheme for purchase of 2 ferry boats	—	—	8,500	
11.	Scheme for supply of Mangalore tiles to replacement of thatched roofs.	36	5	33,930	
12.	Scheme for appointment of Tribal Organizer on honorarium.	4	4	23,000	
			Total Rs.	1,88,930	

I.T.D.P. Gadchiroli No. I Bhamragad, Maharashtra

TABLE 4.3: Expenditure Under Nucleus Budget for the Year 1983-84

Sl. No.	Name of the Scheme	No. of Beneficiaries	No. of Villages	Expenditure Amount	Remarks
1.	Scheme for supply of Agricultural Inputs	50	—	22,327.55	
2.	Scheme for supply of carpets and petromax to 5 *Ghotuls*	—	5	3,000.00	
3.	Scheme for supply of Pre-Primary education to Madia boys	45	13	21,421.06	
4.	Scheme for supply of Primary Education to Madia boys.	33	12	53,399.12	
5.	Scheme for supply of Agricultural Implements	100	10	25,000.00	
6.	Scheme for aiding Adiwasi patients in emergency	—	1	5,000.00	P.H.C., Bhamragad
7.	Scheme for purchase of dresses to dancing troupes	20	—	1,194.30	
8.	Scheme for appointment of tribal organisers on honorarium.	4	4	25,000.00	
			Total Rs.	1,56,332.00	

I.T.D.P. Gadchiroli No. I Bhamragad, Maharashtra

TABLE 4.4: Expenditure Under Nucleus Budget For the Year 1984-85

Sl. No.	Name of the Scheme	No. of Beneficiaries	No. of Villages	Expenditure Amount	Remarks
1.	Scheme for primary education standard I to Madia boys				
		75	19	50,400	
2.	Scheme for primary education standard II to Madia boys				
3.	Scheme for medical facilities to P.H.C., Bhamragad	—	—	5,000	P.H.C., Bhamragad.
4.	Scheme for providing dresses, material to Madia students (Lok Biradari Prakalpa)	250	1	25,000	A.S., Hemalkasa L.B.P.
5.	Scheme for distribution of fruit trees plants	—	—	3,600	
6.	Scheme for tractor ploughing	21	7	11,000	
7.	Scheme for appointment of tribal organizers on honorarium	4	4	29,400	
			Total Rs.	1,24,400	

I.T.D.P. Gadchiroli No. I Bhamragad, Maharashtra

TABLE 4.5: Expenditure Under Nucleus Budget for the Year 1985-86

Sl. No.	Name of the Scheme	No. of Beneficiaries	No. of Villages	Expenditure	Remarks
1.	Scheme for ploughing cultivable land of Madia free of cost	25	7	17,332.35	
2.	Scheme for providing medical facilities to tribal patients	—	2	18,962.20	
3.	Scheme for supply of uniform to tribal children attending Anganwadi/Balwadi.	—	6	24,800.00	
4.	Scheme for organization of community marriage of Madia Adiwasi	10	6	4,519.00	
5.	Scheme for repairing of huts			24,928.00	
6.	—do—	81	22	24,928.00	
7.	—do—			24,928.00	
8.	Scheme for Supply of uniform to tribal students of L.B.P., Hemalkasa	250	1	24,800.00	
9.	Scheme for supply of hospital equipment of L.B.P., Hemalkasa	—	1	25,000.00	
10.	Scheme for supply of Medicines to L.B.P. Hospital, Hemalkasa	—	1	15,000.00	
11.	Scheme for supply of School equipment to L.B.P School, Hemalkasa	—	1	45,000.00	
12.	Appointment of tribal organizer	2	2	15,277.40	
			Total Rs.	2,65,474.95	

I.T.D.P. Gadchiroli No. I Bhamragad, Maharashtra

TABLE 4.6: Nucleus Budget Allotment — Sanctioned Rs. 3 Lakhs for 1986-87

Sl. No.	Name of the Scheme	No. of Beneficiaries	No. of Villages	Provision Amount	Remarks
1	2	3	4	5	6
1.	Scheme for interant on motivation of recruitment of Adiwasi youths	25	—	5,000	Adiwasi youth are appointed as forest guards. Scheme is in progress.
2.	Scheme for training tribal youth in the traditional metal craft	10	2	25,000	
3.	Scheme for loan/subsidy for tribal youth	5	—	15,000	
4.	Scheme for Incentive to the parents of primitive tribal children	40	21	10,000	
5.	Scheme for supply of milk-cans and measuring pot to Madia	25	5	2,000	25 milk cans are supplied
6.	Scheme for bi-cycles to Madia tribals	25	5	14,000	
7.	Scheme for providing medical facilities to Adiwasi patients through Lok-Biradari Prakalpa, Hemalkasa	—	—	25,000	
8.	Scheme for supply of uniforms to the tribal children attending primary school at L.B.P. Hemalkasa	250	6	25,000	

Contd.

TABLE 4.6 *Contd.*

1	2	3	4	5	6
9.	Scheme for supply of uniforms to tribal children attending balwadi	250	6	25,000	
10.	Scheme for supply of uniforms to tribal students of Raje Dharmrao High School, Bhamragad.	80	—	20,000	
11.	Scheme for repair of Adiwasi huts by replacement of Mangalore tiles	27	5	25,000	
12.	Scheme for repair of Adiwasi huts by replacement of Mangalore tiles	27	5	25,000	
13.	Scheme for repair of Adiwasi huts by replacement of Mangalore tiles	27	5	25,000	
14.	Scheme for repair of Adiwasi huts by replacement of Mangalore tiles	27	5	25,000	
15.	Scheme for providing utensils to B.P.L. Adivasi tribal families	40	—	10,000	
16.	Scheme for appointment of tribal organizer	2	—	15,000	2 Tribal Organizers are appointed.
17.	Scheme for organisation of Motivational camps of tribals	80	—	2,000	
Note:	Total amount sanctioned Rs. 3.00 Lakhs.				
	Total schemes approved by the committee of Directors Rs. 2.93 Lakhs.		Total Rs.	2,93,000	

I.T.D.P. Project Officer (Primitive Tribes) Specially at Bhamragad (Distt. Gadchiroli)

Gadchiroli—No. I

TABLE 4.7: Special Central Assistance — 1982-83

Sl. No.	Name of the Scheme	No. of Beneficiaries	No. of Villages	Expenditure Amount	Remarks
1.	Community Hall 5 Nos. *Ghotul* for Madia of Bhamragad	—	5	18,000.00	
2.	Construction of huts with roofing tiles for Madias 100% subsidy	10	12	35,000.00	
3.	Free supply of Agril. inputs, fertilizer of seeds to Madia-Gonds	—	1	5,000.00	
4.	Supply of duster and sprayer to Madia cultivators	9	5	5,000.00	
5.	Schemes for land development for cultivation purpose	1	1	1,000.00	
6.	Supply of Bullock pairs and bullock carts to Madia-Gonds(Carts)	29	14	1,32,087.71	
	(Bullocks)	28			
7.	Supply goat unit	18	8	36,000.00	
8.	Supply of Poultry Birds (100% subsidy)	18			
9.	Supply of Mangalore tiles for replacement of thatched roof	15	3	15,000.00	
10.	Supply of cumbles/carpets 100 Nos. to Madia-Gond families	100	13	20,000.00	
11.	Organization of motivation camp	48	10	1,368.75	
12.	Study tour of Madia Gond in Bhamragad	48	10	15,373.19	
13.	Purchase of Jeep Trolley	—	—	10,170.35	
14.	Construction of C.D. Works	—	—	2,00,000.00	
15.	Construction of staff quarters building/project complex	—	—	5,52,000.00	
16.	Fish farming in impoured water	—	5	50,000.00	
		Total Rs.		10,96,000.00	

I.T.D.P. — Project Officer (Primitive Tribes) Specially at Bhamragad (Distt. Gadchiroli)

TABLE 4.8: Special Central Assistance — 1983-84

Sl. No.	Name of the Scheme	No. of Beneficiaries	No. of Villages	Expenditure Amount	Remarks
1.	Construction of huts to Madia	14	1	70,000.00	
2.	*Construction of community hall (Samaj Mandir)	—	10	50,000.00	*(Mordepar, Korparsi, Dhodraj
3.	Supply of writing material / Uniforms to school-going students	1500	—	47,976.00	Middapalli, Nelgunda, Gundenhod, Bangadi,
4.	Supply of Oil Engine. (one kept in office)	—	—	10,000.00	
5.	Supply of vegetable seed — (Demonstration Plot at Binagunda)	—	1	3,958.85	Tadpari and Kawande)
6.	Supply of bullocks and bullock-carts : Carts	25	10	1,24,505.00	Binagunda, Laheri
	Bullocks	25			
7.	Holding of training camps	—	2	3,284.55	
8.	Study tour of Primitive Tribes	45	11	12,356.95	
9.	Purchase of Tractor Trolley	—	—	1,25,000.00	
10.	Supply of Blankets/carpets to Primitive Tribes	100	13	19,916.82	
11.	Tiling of roofs of huts	36	—	35,928.00	
12.	Construction of Projects Complex at Bhamragad	—	—	4,00,000.00	
13.	Construction of C.D. Works	—	—	2,00,000.00	10 C.D. Works.
14.	Supply of Bullocks	67	—	1,15,984.00	
15.	Supply of Goats	28	—	50,000.00	
16.	Supply of Pigs	—	—	—	
17.	Supply of Breeding Bulls	10	10	40,075.00	
18.	Construction of huts-cum-shelter	6	1	30,000.00	
		Total Rs.		14,14,985.17	

I.T.D.P. – Project Officer (Primitive Tribes) Specially at Bhamragad (Distt. Gadchiroli)

TABLE 4.9: Special Central Assistance — 1984-85

Sl. No.	Name of the Scheme	No. of Beneficiaries	No. of Villages	Expenditure Amount	Remarks
1.	Scheme for supply of Bullocks and Bullock-carts	46	31	2,25,000	
2.	Scheme for fish-farming in impoured water	—	3	71,000	
3.	Scheme for distribution of tiles	106	32	2,00,000	
4.	Scheme for supply of Breeding bullocks	—	8	24,000	
5.	Scheme for distribution of Blankets	909	49	1,00,000	
6.	Construction of Project Complex	—	—	3,35,000	
			Total Rs.	9,55,000	

Note: (1) The A.D.O.Z.P., Gadchiroli supplied 46 bullock pairs but organization of bullock carts have not been reported.
(2) Out of Budget of Rs. Two Lakhs tiles of Rs. One lakhs only were supplied and distributed.

I.T.D.P. — Project Officer (Primitive Tribes) Specially at Bhamragad (Distt. Gadchiroli)

Gadchiroli — No. I

TABLE 4.10: Special Central Assistance — 1985-86

Sl. No.	Name of the Scheme	No. of Beneficiaries	No. of Villages	Expenditure Amount	Remarks
1.	Supply of writing material or dresses to Adiwasi students	—	—	25,000	
2.	Supply of *Ghongadi* (coarse woollen blankets)	133	—	20,000	
3.	Supply of Oil Engine	6	3	56,000	
4.	Supply of bullocks or bullock carts	6	4	2,22,000	
5.	Supply of food for breeding bulls	—	10	24,000	
6.	Animal Husbandry Integrated Project Bhamragad	—	—	1,92,500	
7.	Supply of Milking Animals	29	7	17,800	
8.	Organization of Integrated Staff Project Quarters	—	—	7,00,000	
		Total Rs.		12,57,700	

I.T.D.P. Project Officer (Primitive Tribes) Specially at Bhamragad (Distt. Gadchiroli)

TABLE 4.11: Provision for 1986-87 Special Central Assistance

Sl. No.	Name of the Scheme	Provision	Through
1.	Supply of bullocks and bullock-carts.	2,25,000	A.D.O., Z.P., Gadchiroli.
2.	Establishment of Animal Husbandry Int. Project	6,89,000	Dy. Director, Animal Husbandry, Gadchiroli.
3.	Construction of Animal Husbandry building	3,50,000	— do —
4.	Loan for the Milking Animals	40,000	— do —
5.	Loan for the Poultry birds of Animal Husbandry	31,000	— do —
6.	Loan to the distribution of Goats	9,000	— do —
7.	Supply of breeding bulls	22,000	D.A.H.O., Z.P., Gadchiroli.
8.	Supply of writing material & classes to the Tribal students	30,000	Education Officer, Z.P., Gadchiroli.
9.	Supply of Oil Engines	50,000	T.D.O., Aheri.
10.	Supply of Electric Engines	50,000	— do —
11.	Supply of Ghongadi to the Tribals	20,000	P.O., I.T.D.P., Bhamragad.
	Total	15,16,000	

Abstract

TABLE 4.12: Statement showing the Yearwise Expenditure Under Nucleus Budget: From 1981-82 to 1985-86

Sl. No.	Year	No. of Schemes	Expenditure Rs. Np.	Remarks, if any
1.	1981-82	25	4,49,337.93	
2.	1982-83	12	1,88,930.60	
3.	1983-84	8	1,56,332.03	
4.	1984-85	7	1,24,400.00	
5.	1985-86	13	2,65,474.95	
		Total Rs.	11,84,475.51	

TABLE 4.13: Statement showing the Yearwise Expenditure Under Special Central Assistance From 1982-83 to 1985-86

Sl. No.	Year	No. of Schemes	Expenditure Rs. Np.	Remarks, if any
1.	1982-83	16	10,96,000.00	
2.	1983-84	18	14,14,985.17	
3.	1984-85	6	9,55,000.00	
4.	1985-86	4	12,57,700.00	
		Total Rs.	47,23,685.17	

5

SCREENING OF THE SCHEMES IMPLEMENTED

As stated earlier, the Tribal Sub-Plan strategy envisaged specific schemes for the primitive tribes based on studies carried out on their life situations and problems before planning such schemes. The environmental problems, the level of acculturation of the tribal group and the status of socio-economic conditions were the factors to be considered before finalising such schemes. In Maharashtra State, the Katkaris and the Mādiā-Gonds were the only tribal groups classified as 'primitive', but whereas the Katkaris were only economically backward the Madia-Gonds were classified as being, both, socially and economically primitive and also having a habitation which was not accessible atleast for eight to nine months in an year. Level of awareness was also too low. It is on this background that the schemes detailed in the foregoing pages and their implementation need evaluation.

I

VILLAGE-WISE EVALUATION OF SCHEMES IMPLEMENTED

Factual Position and the Views of Beneficiaries

In this report the statistical analysis of the schemes implemented and the benefits which accrued (or otherwise) is given elsewhere. Figures of expenditure incurred are also given in relevant tables. However an evaluation study of schemes meant for primitive tribals like the Madia-Gonds must concentrate on specific cases which demonstrate the short-comings either of the scheme or of its implementation and also of those schemes which speak of the success. Thus, the description and discussion below assesses the performance of various benefit schemes to highlight the constraints and maladies as well as achievements.

The narrative proceeds village-wise and depicts the facts as observed, verified and the responses, views etc. of the beneficiaries. Situation and environment of the village is also given so as to project difficulties and problems.

The first twenty-two villages are from the Bhamragad (Primitive tribes) Integrated Tribal Development Project Area, followed with ten villages from the Etapalli Project area.

Bhamragad (Primitive Tribes) I.T.D.P. at Bhamragad

1. *Aldandi* (also spelt *Haldandi*)

It is a secluded village about 15 km from Arewada and 22 km from Bhamragad on the north-east of Bhamragad. One has to cross a bad criss-cross dust and boulder laden road and negotiate atleast 4-5 hills. There is almost no traffic and very few trucks ply on the road situated at the centre of big hills, rivers Nibra and Parlakota flow on the other side of the hill and if the hills and rivers are crossed Laheri falls at a distance of about 3-4 km.

The village has 17 houses (thatched huts) and about 120 population. There are no infrastructural facilities and even for fetching drinking water they have to climb the hills and fetch water from a spring. The villagers are left to the whims of nature. Even tiles have not been given to any household. The villagers almost surrounded me and very pathetically argued their case for facilities for the village. An old Madia woman tried to tell so many things. Neither the Project Officer nor any other officer had ever visited this village. I found the conditions in this village worst than that at Binagunda and Kuvvakodi, and, even the level of acculturation and awareness was too low here as compared to Binagunda and Kuvvakodi. Even the solar tube-lights which are installed in villages like Hemalkasa, Bhamragad, Laheri etc. are not seen here. In fact such far-off secluded villages should have been given priority. Probably, the road-side villages are good for 'window-dressing' and publicity.

Tiles for roofing have been given to six households (out of whom one has left the village), pair of bullocks to two and pair of bullocks plus bullock-cart to two persons.

The people demanded bullocks and bullock-carts Anganwadi and Balwadi for their children and a dispensary.

Peka Poriya Madkami – the *Gayata* (Patel) of the village, impatiently asked whether their village will get things or not? A Madia student from other village viz. Lalsu Malu Timma who had come as a guest and was a 11th class commerce student at the College at Aheri was present at the time of interviews and discussions.

2. *Arewada*

Village is about 8 km from Bhamragad. Pairs of bullocks, bullock-carts and tiles for roofing have been distributed in the village.

One person was sanctioned Rs. 2,000 for brick-making.

Uniforms for Anganwadi children half shirt and pant for boys and skirts for girls have been distributed. The total amount spent during 1985-86 being Rs. 24,800 which sounds too high. The attendance at Anganwadi is about 35-40 but the attendance is more due to the nutritive food given than for schooling. The village is about 8 km from Bhamragad and as such shows some higher accul- turation.

In all, ten beneficiaries under different schemes were interviewed and all except one had actually received the benefits. Shri Shankar Vistari Kumre who was sanctioned Rs. 2,000 for brick-making (through the M.S. Tribal Development Corporation, Sub-Regional Office at Aheri) was shown to have been received the benefit by the sub-regional office of the M.S.T.D.C. during 1985-86, actually the concerned person had not taken the amount till 22nd April, 1987. (This discrepancy was brought to the notice of the Sub-Regional Manager, M.S.T.D.C., Aheri, who explained that the benefit was 'granted' but was not actually distributed and the name was included in the list supplied through oversight).

3. *Bhamragad (Tole)*

This being the central village and the Project office Headquarters, different types of schemes were implemented here. There is a High School with Hostel, Animal Husbandry Project of the State Government, Anganwadi, Primary Health Centre, M.S.T.D. Corporation's office with a Manager and a warehouse, Range Forest

Office and a Post Office. A few private shops (of the nature of departmental stores catering to various needs), small hotels located in huts etc. – are also available. A Fisher-mens' Cooperative Society is also active and its President Shri Dunga Irpa Gumma appeared to be an aware and hardworking individual. Solar power tube lights have been installed at three places with good results. Each tube-light was reported to cost around Rs. 25,000.

Various schemes implemented included the usual ones e.g. tiles for roofing, pair of bullocks, bullock-carts, etc. However other schemes included distribution of oil engines for irrigation, sewing machines with training in tailoring, loans for opening cycle-shop (for giving cycles on rent), vegetable shops, one month's training to tribals in Animal Husbandry with a stipend of Rs. 300 p.m. and one cow with one calf and six goats (cost to be returned within five years) supply of *(Prakashtha Upkaran)* earth-work implements like axe, spade, pick axe, iron pan, crow-bar etc.

Training for seeking jobs in civil services, distribution of uniforms to Anganwadi children and uniforms for the High School students, provision of two Ferry boats on the rivers at Bhamragad and supply of Fish-seed were the general schemes implemented. The list provided also showed one beneficiary who was showed to have been given Rs. 2,000 (844-85/N.B.) for brick-making and Rs. 1,000 for bricks and tile making to another beneficiary. However no such persons could be traced nor any one knew of any such brick-making or tile-making units.

A scheme named 'repairs to huts' (through P.O.) was actually supply of tiles for roofing which is already a general scheme of the P.O. under N.B.

Waman Lachmaji Uike (Son of Bhamragad *Sarpanch*) has been granted a loan of Rs. 5,000 Grocery Shop during 1985-86, and he has received half the amount, however the shop had not been started till May 1987. He says he has kept the amount safe in Bank and shall start the grocery-shop on getting sum on crop season.

The vegetable-shop of Shri Laxman Mengji Veladi who was granted a loan of Rs. 1,000 in 1985-86 from N.B. has not been opened nor has he taken the amount. It was also reported that he has left Bhamragad and is at Dhodraj.

When enquiries were made at the Sub-Regional Office of M.S.T.D.C. at Aheri, through their Manager at Bhamragad, they told that names were included in the list supplied through oversight.

The sewing machines given to two beneficiaries – one of them a girl, are being used by them and they could support their families from the income. Some training in tailoring was also given to the girl. (The other beneficiary already knew tailoring).

The fish-seed *(Matsyabeej)* was spread in the ponds/lakes at Hemalkasa and Malampoddur (as there is no water in the lake at Bhamragad) and the members of the Fishermens' Cooperative Society who are trained at the training course organised by the Society reap the fish harvest. Dunga Irpa Gumma President of the Society told that the scheme proved useful. He also told that the two ferry-boats (1986-87 from P.O.) were expected within a week i.e. by 28th April, 1987.

In the case of Ramsha Koksha Madavi who was given an oil engine for irrigation, the engine was not found with him and he told that he has given it on hire to others (he said 'to an employee of the Forest Deptt.'). The reason given by him was that he could not get diesel for using the engine. It is very interesting to note that throughout the I.T.D.P. Bhamragad area there is no Petrol-pump. The Allapalli Petrol-pump is 62 kms. from Bhamragad and almost all I.T.D.P. area/villages are ahead of Bhamragad. Even at Allapalli Petrol-pump, diesel is mostly out of stock. The developmental agencies distributing oil engines have not made any arrangements for providing diesel. After enquiry it was gathered that the only source of getting diesel was from the employees of the Forest Department or Ballarpur Industries – which obviously is an 'illegal' source of diesel. It is interesting to note that the oil engine scheme of the Government is virtually dependent for its success on a 'No. 2' source of diesel and there is no official provision in the scheme for making available the fuel and it has now become a premium on one of its own (Forest) department. It was reported that by way of compensation for obliging the beneficiary the employees either charge at Rs. 6-8 per litre of diesel or use the engine for their personal purpose. (Then the price of diesel was Rs. 2.25 per litre.)

The cycle-shop of Shri Keshav Chinna Madavi to whom five 'Avon' cycles were given is at Tadgaon which is about 8-10 kms. from Bhamragad on the main road towards Etapalli. Technically the cycle-hire shop started by him should have been located at Bhamragad, however Tadgaon is a place which is the main village for reaching Bhamragad and during rainy season there is no other means of communication except a bi-cycle. To that extent this is justified.

He is getting good business. So the cycles have helped him and others in the area.

Mangru Chaitu Madavi alias Gota was sanctioned a pair of bullocks in 1984-85, but he has not received the bullocks though the list supplied mentions that benefit was given. He was first called to Laheri, then to Bhamragad but till (22-4-87) he had not received the pair. The Sub-Regional Manager T.D.C. at Aheri informed that the benefit was granted but yet to be distributed, though it was included in the list supplied through mistake.

Shri Sitaramji Sadmek an Ex-*Sarpanch*, about 85 years old was critical of the schemes. He said the Project Office distributes Bullocks and carts to those who already have these things. There are some who have land but no means to cultivate; and they don't get it. There are two 'propogandists' (the term used by him for the 'Organisers') viz. Mr. T. and Mr. P. 'through whom' only these benefits can be obtained. Shri Sadmek said that he had a plan of cultivating vegetables for which he had been trying to get an oil engine for the last 3-4 years. But he could not get one, because to quote him, "*hum khushamat nahi karte*".

The Primary Health Centre at Bhamragad has a doctor but no medicines. In the old Chandrapur district there used to be medicines but no Doctor, according to Shri Sadmek, since the establishment of Gadchiroli district 'there has been a doctor but no medicines and the unit is neglected'.

4. *Bangadi*

A remote village for which one has to walk on foot through a hilly tract on the side slopes of Gundenhod is a Bada Madia village where shifting cultivators were settled. A village of eleven houses, it lacks infrastructural facilities. Six beneficiaries got tiles for the roofing of their houses. Tiles have been given to the Ghotul however the scheme shown in the statement is of building community centre under the S.C.A. during 1983-84 (Rs. 5000 each).

The various facilities required are not available in this village. Five persons have been given pairs of bullocks and only two got bullock-carts. One youth viz. Gudsa Dura Parsa had an opportunity to go with a tour organised by the Project Officer to Nagpur, Chandrapur, Warora (Anandwan) etc. The boy was extremely happy over the experience and I found him to be jubilant, intelligent and smart. He narrated of having met Baba Amte at Anandwan and seen poultry at Nagpur.

5. *Binagunda*

Eighteen km from Laheri towards East (on the Laheri-Kuvvakodi road) is Binagunda, for reaching which one has to negotiate a series of big hills, with bad roads, steep inclines which makes it a dusty and a bit risky drive. Except the bamboo loaded trucks of the Ballarpur Industries Ltd. there is no other traffic. There are intercepting rivers and *nullas* where there are no bridges/rafts etc. and big and small rounded, granite boulders in the basin pose a formidable threat to the drum and engine of the jeep. However the scenic beauty on the sides of the roads amply compensates the strain of the journey. Situated on a plateau and surround by hilly tracks the small village of Binagunda is an abode of the so-called Bada-Madia or Bhera Madia (Bhera-Behra means 'Bada') who are known to be at a lower level of acculturation as compared to the so-called Chota-Madias on the plains below. These Bada Madias are hill loving and living people and hence are also called 'Meta' (means Hill) Madias and are traditionally shifting cultivators (called 'Penda' in Madia dialect). The Government claims to have stopped shifting cultivating but as will be shown below it is still in vogue in the area though on a small scale.

Binagunda with a cool climate has been an experimental land for the project schemes. All the previous and present Project Officers have been visiting Binagunda and have concentrated on this village. Even the Secretary/Commissioner, Collectors, other visitors have been frequently visiting the place and are shown the demonstrations. Lime light and publicity thus hover over Binagunda.

A village with eighteen houses it has a population of about 75 who are Bada-Madias. Shri Sayabi Kana Durva, the Gayata (Patel) of Binagunda is an enthusiastic, smart person, who has working knowledge of Hindi/Marathi and was participant of a tour organised by the Project Officer to Bombay and other places. Thus he has became alert and hence could take initiative in persuading his village people development oriented.

We shall examine the group schemes implemented at Binagunda.

Demonstration Plots: During 1981-82, 1982-83 when Shri Gaikwad was the Project Officer demonstration forms on irrigation were started wherein ground-nut, cucumbers, onions, brinjals, gourds, tobacco, tomatoes, chillies, ridged-gourds etc. were planted. Even banana, papayya etc. were planted. Many people have the fruit trees in their kitchen garden. Presently the demonstration plot of ground-nut, brinjals, tobacco, chilli, onions etc. is being grown by the Forest Department. While asked the Gayata and others from the village said that, "we like all these products and will also grow the crops but we don't get the seeds and irrigation facility". They eat banana and papayya and both raw-as vegetables and ripe fruits.

A health-camp for Madia tribals was held in 1983-84, which is mentioned in P.O.'s records as 'Madia Shibir'.

Mineral mixture for feeding the bullocks was supplied in 1981-82 to 19 persons.

An organiser was appointed by P.O. during 1985-86 viz. Mr. P. who has now left Binagunda and usually resides at Dhodraj.

Two youth received training in Animal Husbandry for one month, stipend of Rs. 300 and are expecting to receive a cow. The two boys said they will drink milk after getting the cow.

Seventeen families (i.e. almost all families) were given pairs of bullocks but about 13 pairs died due to diseases. The veterinary doctor pays visits very rarely. Two months back he had come which was after a gap of 2-3 years after distribution of bullocks.

Roofing tiles were given for the Ghotul and for ten persons. The Gayata said that they want to widen the Ghotul and hence need more tiles. Similarly eight families did not get tiles. He felt, all should be given the benefit.

The Gayata (Patel) Sayabi Kana Durva received an oil engine in 1986-87 which never worked, when this was reported by him to the P.O. Bhamragad he was told that he will arrange for taking it back, which has not been done so far (25-4-87). The functionaries of the Forest Department tried to use it for their own work using their diesel but the engine did not work. So it is lying unused with the Gayata.

Four boys and three girls participated in the trip to Nagpur and other places arranged by P.O. during 1986-87 and reported to have seen Circus, Railway train, Aeroplane, poultry farm and ate at big Hotels at Nagpur. They enjoyed the trip and became aware of modern life. All participants were happy and appeared jubilant over the things seen. They wanted to see other places.

Brass utensils and alluminium utensils were given to the families which are of good quality and include the brass ganj (Big), 2 alluminium ganj, *(Handa)* two plates, one aluminium lid *(Dhakkan)*, bowls 3 *(Katorya)*, and one woollen blanket. These were physically verified and appeared to be of good quality and kept neat and clean though being used.

The Gayata used the work 'Sirganti' (Census) and a youth suggested that their farms should be ploughed not only by tractors but "bulldozers" should be used. (The Ballarpur Industries Ltd., Ballarpur, has its depot near Binagunda. They also render services to the Madias due to which they know their huge machines etc.).

Thus at a remote place between high hills, Binagunda seems to be a village with a better level of understanding and awareness and better acculturation. This is probably due to a concentration of schemes here resulting in frequent visits of the P.O. other higher officers and better exposure of the people to all these things. (A useful 'window dressing' too?).

The Gayata was all praise for the late Shri M.D. Pathak who was Project Officer and for the Collector and Shri Lalfak Zuvela, Tribal Commissioner of Maharashtra, who had recently visited the village (on 15-4-87).

The Gayata demanded expansion of Ghotul, reclaimation of land by using Bulldozers and tractors, pairs of bullocks for all households paddy seeds and rice for domestic consumption etc. He informed that 'Penda' (shifting cultivation) was stopped in Binagunda (not to be fully believed by us) but was in progress in Turemarka, Fodewada, Timeli and Kuvvakodi. He praised Shri Agrawal of B.I.L.T. (Ballarpur Industries Pvt. Ltd.).

The Gaita also referred to a survey conducted some time back (during his father's regime' as a Gaita) which he said was conducted by the then Project Officer Shri Pathak and Shri Raj Reddy (a contractor with philanthropic and socially oriented attitude who resides at Hyderabad whose name is known to many in the area). This probably was a reference to the pioneering work for preparing a project proposal report for this primitive tribes area which was done by Late Shri M.D. Pathak which the then Collector J. Joseph describes in his foreword to the Project-Report as "comprehensive and encompasses all the identified needs of primitive Madias". Shri Pathak died of cerebral Malaria which was dominant in that area.

6. *Bodange*

About 12 km from Gotpadi going to the south-west of Gotpadi is a small village Bodange. The roads are bad and route circutous, so much so that but for the guidance of Gogga Gaita of Gotpadi who accompanied us, we might have been lost in the forest and confused: The total number of houses is 15 and the population is about 75. Not a single house i.e. hut in the village has tiles on roof. Tiles have not been given to this village. Pairs of bullocks were given to two persons from S.C.A. during 1984-85 and one person obtained a bullock-cart i.e. cart only in 1985-86 (from N.B.). The cart is fairly good but completely of non-teak wood. Bodange is a village where shifting cultivators were settled by the social welfare department during 1963-64. It was observed that such villages (also Gotpadi) which are, popularly called 'Sarkari' villages have not been given much benefits under the T.S.P. schemes. The reason for this step-motherly treatment could not be known. The fact that they were given benefit when settled should not mean that they don't need anything in future. The people were demanding tiles for roofing, pairs of bullocks, carts, cycles etc. Drinking water is not available, hence the villagers demanded a tube-well at Bodange and one more at the Tola of Bodange.

7. *Dhodraj*

Between Bhamragad and Laheri, at about 7 km from Bhamragad is village Dhodraj. Being relatively a big village various schemes were implemented. It has a mixed population which includes Madias, Gonds, Pardhans and a few non-tribals viz. Telis.

The general schemes implemented included providing tiles for the roof of Ghotul, building 'Samaj Mandir' (Community Centres) distribution of uniforms to Anganwadi children, ploughing of farms by tractor, training in Animal Husbandry, distribution of milk-cans/ kettles, distribution of decorative articles for dancing troupes etc.

Roofing tiles were given for the Ghotul. This was verified and found to be done.

A 'Samaj Mandir' has been built during 1984-85 under S.C.A. and was ready, and since the last one year, State Reserve Police outpost has been posted in the building. The place was visited and it was seen that the construction of the building is bad. The flooring and walls have developed cracks, material used is extremely useless. The S.R.P. men told that since last year when they occupied the building (then it was new) the condition is the same.

Regarding the ploughing by tractor, the beneficiaries were not satisfied because, they said, the soil was so hard that tractor could not work. The driver tried one round and then went away. In all six beneficiaries got this benefit, the ploughing ranging between two to five acres per beneficiary during 1985-86 from N.B. They again ploughed it with traditional method.

The dancing troupe of boys and girls got items like blouse, shirts, ribbons, cosmetic items, musical bells (*Ghungru*), bead-necklaces etc.

The Animal Husbandry unit at Bhamragad trained Madia youths for one month and paid a stipend of Rs. 300 per head. Later they were given one cow, one calf, one she-goat. In few cases the cow died. It seems that the type/breed of cow given is unsuitable for the climate and environment. It does not get sufficient grass. The amount of Insurance for the cow was taken away by the concerned authorities.

Milk-cans/kettles were given from N.B. to those who were given cows. A follow-up scheme taken up during 1986-87 was to provide cycles to such individuals so that they can distribute/sale milk at places like Bhamragad. Thus training in Animal Husbandry giving a cow with calf, she-goats, milk-cans cycles appears to be a well-linked scheme. However the cycles were yet (May 1987) to be given to all and they are demanding cycles. The P.O. said that he is expecting consignment.

The usual schemes of tiles for roofing, pair of bullocks and carts etc. were also implemented. But it was reported and verified that the quality of tiles supplied was bad and after the first rain many tiles gave way (i.e. they were not properly backed).

A very interesting case of loan on fifty per cent subsidy for purchase of brooms' (the terms 'purchase' '*Zaroo Kharidi*' used by the M.S.T.D.C. seems to be defective, probably it should be 'preparation of brooms and sale') was investigated. the M.S. Tribal Development Corporation had reported to have given Rs. 500 during 1984-85 (as per the statement supplied by them) to one Smt. Povari Masa Kovasa, a Madia woman of Dhodraj. When the woman was personally contacted, she was surprised to know this as she neither aspired nor applied for such an amount, nor did she receive any amount for broom-purchase from any source. She even added that she does not want any amount for any such purpose. There is no other woman by this name in the village.

Smt. Rukmabai Gosai Sedam was given an oil engine by T.D.O. Aheri during 1984-85. She is using the engine for growing vegetables and growing brinjals, onions, chillies etc. She was satisfied and gets good income. Even here it was reported by the beneficiary that the source of diesel is from Forest Department or the workers of Ballarpur Industries.

An interesting scheme was, 'supply of utensils for Family welfare' (*Kutumb Kalyan Ke Liye Bartan*). The scheme was implemented by P.O. Shri Mangru Maida Michhya got the benefit. He got himself operated for vasectomy. Some utensils were given as an incentive for getting oneself operated. In this case the amount from I.T.D.P. funds was utilised for supply of those utensils. This cannot be considered to be a good scheme, when the government is already having its routine incentive schemes for this purpose.

Bande Budga Mohanda an old man of about 70, lost his eyesight after an operation for cataract. Only one eye works but sight is very weak. A very influential Madia from the village, he told that the Organiser Mr. P. takes Rs. 2 for writing applications of beneficiaries for getting benefits under various schemes. He also told that those who offered Toddy, Chicken etc. to Mr. P. could get the benefit.

As per the list supplied a Fair-Price Shop was granted to one Shri Kutta Dasru Pungati of Dhodraj (and also a milk-can). This man was out of station for many days and no such shop could be found in the village. His wife is local Anganwadi worker but she was also out of station, probably (as reported) they had taken their child to a dispensary at Allapalli.

The parents of the children from Anganwadi told that uniforms were distributed to Anganwadi children during 1985-86 (N.B.).

8. *Gongwada*

Five km away in forest from Gotpadi i.e. about twelve kms. from Dhodraj (which is on the main-Bhamragad-Laheri Road) is village Gongwada. It is a small village and very few schemes have been implemented here.

In one case tiles were given to Malu Kopa Modyami but were actually received by Chaitu Gilla Pungati. The original beneficiary did not lodge any complaint.

Kopa Modyami was given a bullock-cart, but without bullocks i.e. only cart. He had no bullocks. As a result he signed, (i.e. made thumb impression) on the receipt but actually did not bring the cart as he said 'what is the use of a cart without bullocks? Such typical cases were found in some other villages also. When the poor Madias had applied for getting pairs of bullocks *and* a bullock cart some were given *only carts*. They said that if only bullocks are given they could atleast plough the land but with a cart only they could not do anything. The concerned officers should have known that when the beneficiary did not have bullocks 'putting a cart before bullocks' was useless.

Many Madias demanded tiles for roofing, bullocks and bullock-cart, and demanded oil-engine.

9. *Gotpadi*

About seven km to the south-west of Dhodraj is village Gotpadi which is one of the places where shifting cultivators were settled in 1961-62. They call it a 'Sarkari' village. Having a back-drop of hills, this was our camp for a few days. It has 12 houses and population is around 70.

Not a single household got tiles for roofing. Even the Ghotul is in a bad condition. Tiles have not been given for repairs of the Ghotul. The villages contributed for Ghotul tiles. The Gaita of the village Shri Gogga Kohla Pungati told that they had demanded ploughing of land by tractor, but nothing was done. Bullock-carts were given to two beneficiaries (1985-86) and pair of bullocks to one beneficiary (1984-85). There is one tube-well in the village.

There is a primary school with classes up to 4th primary standard. But there are students only in the 1st and 2nd standard. It is a one-teacher school run by Zilla Parishad. Shri D.J. Warwade is the teacher. He is a young man who attended two training programmes in Madia-dialect and culture organised by the State Institute of Educational Research & Training, Pune through the Zilla Parishad at Aheri and Gadchiroli during 1985-86 and 1986-87 respectively. He said that the training proved helpful. The teacher has to go to Etapalli for getting his salary. During rainy season the village is cut-off and going or coming back becomes a problem. In fact the disbursement of salary could and should be done at Bhamragad at the Project Office and the P.C.B.D.O. Etapalli can easily send an accountant there for a couple of days. It is interesting to note that on record there are two T.D. Blocks under the Etapalli Panchayat Samiti viz. Etapalli and Bhamragad, but the Bhamragad Block is only on paper. At least under the above circumstances the Bhamragad Headquarters can be used for intermittent services like the one cited above.

Mr. P., the organiser appointed by Project Officer was reported to have visited the village many times and collected money at the rate of Rs. 2 from all prospective beneficiaries telling them that this was the (his) fee for writing application but later nothing came out. This complaint was heard in a few more villages.

The villagers had some problems and the administration did not pay attention. Shri Warvade the teacher helped a few villagers by writing applications for them. He was telling that there was a talk that he is making the villagers 'aware' and indulging in 'politics'. As a matter of fact the real role of a teacher in such remote, backward villages is to make them aware and assist them in getting their due from the development administration. That is the central theme of Adult Education programme and the Community/Tribal development schemes. (I had an occasion to meet his Inspector (A.D.I,) Shri G.S.B. (I/c of Bhamragad beat) and I told him to look into the matter).

Tractor ploughing: Regarding the ploughing of fields with tractor the people felt that once this was done but later there was no follow-up. They said that ploughing by tractor in one stray year is not helpful. It should be a continuing benefit. When I asked the Gaita and others that as per their tradition ploughing of land (by any means) was tabooed and they were 'shifting cultivators' till they were settled in this village, and on this background how is it that they accept ploughing by tractor? The reply was they, "the old 'Jamana' has now gone", and that, "we have accepted the new ideas so we want ploughing every year". He even agreed to have a consolidated ploughing programme for all villagers so that the work can be done in a short span of time. The attitudinal change in the traditional outlook and acceptance of the new technology is very clear. The government should utilise the community living spirit in the Madias, indicated in the above suggestion. If the Gaita and villagers meet and give a suitable compact programme, ploughing could be economical and faster.

The bullock-cart (i.e. cart only) given to a beneficiary was examined. The wheels and the axis were of old wood (as if it was used for years) and the rest of the wood looked new. Cracks had developed on wheels and axis. As per the list supplied, the cart is given to him in 1985-86, but was actually brought from the Project Office in April 1987 which explains the reason behind old wheels and axle. However, because he has no bullocks cart is not used.

Grass or Shindi leaves are not available in or around the village. The people demanded Bullocks and carts and tiles for roofing and ploughing of land by tractor.

10. *Gundenhod*

Twenty-four km from Bhamragad and about 5 km from Laheri is Gundenhod for which one has to cross a hill and a nulla named Ogwe. A small village of eight houses the population is around fifty. Village has a picturesque natural background of hills etc. but no infrastructural facilities. These are the Bada Madia tribals who were dissuaded from shifting cultivation and settled in 1960-61, however some of them still practise it.

A plantation plot has been developed as a demonstration plot by Ballarpur Industries and groundnut, tobacco, brinjals, onions etc. were seen growing. The products go to the local Madias.

The list provided by the P.O. Office shows that during 1983-84 under S.C.A. a 'Samaj Mandir' (Community Centre) was built at Gundenhod, however there *is no such Samaj Mandir* and the villagers reported that tiles on the roofing of the Ghotul were replaced and the amount was given by the P.O. It must be noted that there was another scheme under which Ghotuls were built/repaired or tiles supplied for Ghotuls. It is queer to find out that while at two other places (viz. Dhodraj and Nelgunda) Samaj Mandirs were actually constructed – however bad and dilapilated they may be – at Gundenhod no such structure is seen and the only thing visible was tiles on the Ghotul roof.

Roofing tiles, bullocks, carts, etc. were given. Only three houses have not received tiles or bullocks. Karya Vatte Pungati reported that one of the bullocks died for want of medical aid, and he could not take the bullock to Bhamragad as the distance is too much. Veterinary Doctor does not pay visits.

Vatte Kotla Vadde got an oil engine during 1984-85 and has been using it. He takes water from the Ogwe nulla and irrigates land.

However diesel is not available and he added to say that money for purchasing diesel is also not available.

There are many Charoli (Chironji) trees but collection and processing of Charoli was not practised.

11. *Hemalkasa*

I. Hemalkasa Lok-Biradari Prakalpa

Two km prior to Bhamragad is the famous Lok-Biradari Prakalpa of Shri Baba Amte, Magsasay Award Winner Leprosy Worker from Anandwan, Warora. The Maharogi Seva Samiti (a Public Trust) is the parent body and Shri Baba Amte's younger son Dr. Prakash Amte (M.B.B.S.) and his wife Dr. Mr. Manda Amte manage this Prakalpa. Treatment to and rehabilitation of the leprosy patients is the main purpose; however through their well-equipped hospital they are also rendering medical services to the Madia tribals in the area. The originally superstitious Madias who depended upon the Bhagats and their black-magic, herbal medicines etc. have, started believing in the allopathic medicines and cure which is a significant-attitudinal and behavioural change in the community and is of great magnitude.

The Biradari also runs a school for tribal children and has co-related activities like nursery, a Zoo etc.

The P.O. has given substantial grants to the Lok-Biradari Prakalpa during 1982-83 to 1986-87 making provision from the nucleus budget. The schemewise details are given in Table 5.1.

Table 5.1 shows that expenditure on the item of school uniforms is too high, (compared to the amount spent by P.O.) coming as it is to about Rs. 100 per student (See Table 5.6). Two half pants and half-shirts (for boys) and skirts and blouse (for girls) were supplied (of cotton fibre). About writing equipment also the average comes to Rs. 180 per student.

The expenditure on hospital equipment and medicines was fully utilised for tribal beneficiaries. An interesting thing was reported. Initially (may be up to 1984-85) the P.O. used to contact the L.B.P. people at the fag end of financial year and offer grant from N.B. – probably to fulfil expenditure target. Later the L.B.P. workers requested the P.O. to inform them in advance and give N.B. grant as per 'their' requirements. As a result, the P.O. formulated the schemes (under column 1 and 2) in which material/equipment or medicines were to be supplied as per needs.

TABLE 5.1: Schemes implemented through grants to Lok-Biradari Prakalpa, Hemalkasa

Year	Equipment/Material for the Dispensary as per needs	Schemes: Medicines for the Dispensary as per needs	Schemes: Uniform to the School Students	Writing (School) equipment for School students
1	2	3	4	5
1982-83	—	—	25,000.00 (216 students)	—
1983-84	—	—	—	—
1984-85	—	—	25,000.00 (250 students)	—
1985-86	25,000.00	15,000.00	24,800.00 (250 students)	45,000-00 (250 students)
1986-87		24,852.50 (1125 Benes)	24,948.00 (275 students)	—
	25,000.00	39,852.50	99,748.00	45,000.00

Based on their experience of working among and in the interest of tribals Shri Vilas Manohar of the L.B.P. offered the following suggestions regarding the T.S.P. schemes *vis-a-vis* the tribal beneficiaries in the area:

(i) Going all the way to the doorstep of tribals and offering benefits encourages bad tendency. They must be asked to do something, work or pay a part thereof. It may be that roofing tiles etc. may be given but not all the things. e.g. If the village takes up tree plantation, utensils, cycle pump etc. may be given.
(ii) The community spirit of the village and Ghotul could be used. Giving utensils for the whole village and keeping them in Ghotul with the Gaita will be in community interest. This will not give rise to bickerings and internal strife/politics which comes through individual benefits.
(iii) For deciding 'Below Poverty level' not the acrage of land owned but the output should be considered.
(iv) In Abhujmar (M.P.) the P.O. has many powers. In

Maharashtra, though the post of P.O. is class I, equivalent to Deputy Collector, he acts just as a 'post-office' for distributing tiles, bullock-carts etc. coming from subject-matter departments and keeps paper records. He must be entrusted with powers to protect the socio-economic aspects of tribals' life. If tribals are exploited he should be competent to act and stop it. He should keep a vigil on situation and thwart exploiters. At Mirgudwancha a forest officer insists on liquor from tribals or harasses them. The P.O. should have powers to check him.

(v) For *post-mortem* the body has to be taken to Aheri, *post-mortem* should be possible at Bhamragad. Presently the Police ask the Madias to carry the body to Aheri. At times the body is putrifying and the whole ordeal is harassing to the tribals.

(vi) Teachers' salaries clould be disbursed at Bhamragad. The issue of National Savings Certificates and payments against such certificates also could be arranged at Bhamragad post-office.

(vii) During 1982-83 the Adivasi Cooperative Societies (A.C.S.) purchased paddy from the Madia tribals and before making payments went into liquidation. The concerned Madias have not received payments for their paddy till today. Who will pay it? Without recommendation of the A.C.S. which are now defunct the farmers don't get loans. Why should be P.O. not empowered to recommend cases in lieu of the A.C.S. which are non-existent.

II. Hemalkasa Village

About two kilometres away from the Lok-Biradari Prakalpa is the Hemalkasa village. Solar tube-lights are erected on roads in this village.

Apart from usual schemes of tiles for roofing, bullock-carts etc. the scheme of ploughing land by tractors was also implemented. As there were no rains the farmers could not express opinion about the advantages of tractor-ploughing.

If they get labour work then bullock-cart is used as carrier and they earn money. The cart was of mixed wood, the main posts *(Dhura)* being of teak-wood and rest of it being of lesser quality wood.

The villagers in general were not very enthusiastic about the benefits accrued or about demanding new benefits. While asked they did not specify which benefits will they need in future.

Fish-seed was provided and it was put in the Hemalkasa lake, the members of the Fishermens' Cooperative Society, Bhamragad took the benefit and got fishes (a corporate benefit scheme).

12. *Hiddur*

Six kilometres from Arewada and fourteen kilometres to the north of Bhamragad is Hiddur, which is a village where the Bada-Madia shifting cultivators were settled by the Government.

A small village which lacks many facilities, only the scheme of distribution of tiles for roofing (400 + 30 tiles) was implemented that too in a queer manner. They were told that only those who will undergo family planning operation will get the tiles. Hence all interviewed beneficiaries told that they got themselves operated and then only the tiles were given. This is a strange way of linking of a benefit given under Special Central Assistance with the 'target' fulfilment of family planning. It amounts to an extorting behaviour and is against the philosophy and our accepted methods of development, that too when it is done in case of a primitive tribe.

Under another scheme implemented viz. repairs to huts, only tiles were given.

All the inhabitants were demanding bullocks and bullock-carts. Oil engines were also demanded by those who have rivulets under their farms. Here again one Koriya Dunga Durva got a cart but has no bullocks so he said he is unable to use the benefit. Cycle was also demanded by a few persons.

While asked about 'Penda' (shifting cultivation) they said they have given it up and the settled method is better. A couple of persons nad gone to hills for shifting cultivation but have returned to Hiddur. I had visited this village in 1975-76 *but even after eleven 'development' years the conditions are almost the same*, may be because it is a 'Sarkari' village.

13. *Hitapadi*

About 2-3 kilometres before Aldandi between Arewada and Aldandi is Hitapadi, a small villages.

Here again tiles for roofing were given on the same condition that only those who get operated for family planning will get the tiles.

Those who did it got tiles. But one Povari Narango Pungati complained that he got himself operated and even then tiles were not yet given to him.

Karve Narango Pungati and Narango Kovala Pusali got bullocks and cart and bullock-cart respectively. Karve Narango Pungati wanted implements for starting Black-smithy and tiles. Out of them Narango Kovala Pusali left the village and went to Dirangi on hills but later returned to Hitapadi.

Others from the village wanted tiles, bullocks, cart etc.

14. *Juvvi*

About six kilometres to the south of Dhodraj is village Juvvi.

Tiles, bullocks and carts have been given to a few villages.

Milk-cans and cycles have been distributed to those who have been given cows. The boys had one month's training in Animal Husbandry at Bhamragad and each of them got a cow, a calf etc.

Cycles were given in March 1987. Cycle is of 'Hero' company and on physical verification and a trial ride appeared to be a good one. Cycles have been given on 20 per cent contribution basis i.e. the beneficiary pays Rs. 130 and Rs. 500 are given by the P.O. from S.C.A. funds.

One Pusu Geba Pungati, a Madia youth of 20-22 years got tiles, training in Animal Husbandry with a stipend of Rs. 300, a cow, milk can and cycle. The cow has gone very weak and does not yield milk as per expectations hardly 0.5 litre twice (We actually saw the cow). Tiles have been given on 50 per cent subsidy basis. So he paid Rs. 200 for which regular receipt has been passed. There is very little income from the cow and he is not in a good financial condition. Consequently it is difficult for him to pay back the loan, though there is no fixed time limit. He told that the Forest Department (under their scheme) allotted a bullock-cart to him, but as it was of a very bad quality he did not accept it. *The officials persuaded him to take it away but* he *did not* (He also did not give signature indicative of the receipt of the article which some other Madias in other villages had done).

Mr. P. the organiser appointed by the P.O. was reported to have collected about Rs. 200 for writing applications for the whole village at the rate of Rs. 2 per application per benefit scheme.

15. *Kiyar*

About eight kilometres from Hemalkasa is Kiyar, known for the traditional metal art of the Otankars. There is an Anganwadi at Kiyar and villagers told that uniforms were distributed to children. However the Anganwadi worker was not there since March 1987 and they reported that she is sick. Consequently we could not visit it. Under the scheme of 'Repairs to huts', actually repairs were not done which again meant that only tiles were given. Here also beneficiaries told that only those who were operated for family planning received tiles. But almost all had already operated. Even a lady Smt. Gomi Pandhri Madavi who received tiles (for 'hut repairs') had also an F.P. operation performed.

Other schemes included distribution of pair of bullocks, bullock-carts, oil engines etc.

Oil-engine: Shri Guna Peka Kudyeti got an oil engine in 1983-84 from T.D.O. Aheri. He said that as the spanners, pipe and diesel were not given it could not be used. There is a river near his land but about 250 feet pipe is required. This was not supplied. Hence he got the pipe on hire twice but this was not always possible. The mechanic from Lok-Biradari Prakalpa, Hemalkasa helped in installation and commissioning of the pump. When I asked to show the pump and though persistently said that I can even walk down the bad-land he was reluctant to take us to his farm though he insisted that it is very much there. I believe that the pump has been given by him to someone on hire atleast temporarily. He demanded, pipe, spanners, deepening and bunding of the *'Bodi'* (small lake) near his farm etc. Due to the above problems he could not get much benefit from the pump which he knows he can, provided accessories are made available.

Metal-work Training: Another general scheme which was implemented during 1982-83 was giving training to Madia in Metal-work — the indigenous art of the village. The 'Otankars' prepare pots, idols, decorative articles from brass and copper; which is their traditional art. I interviewed an old man (aged about 90 years) Shri Bandu Vanga Madavi — an Otankar by caste — was the teacher at the training which was organised at Bhamragad during 1982-83, and started in September 1982. The duration was of six months. He told the trainees were given stipend at Rs. 200 per month, for six months. Later, they were supposed to get Rs. 5,000 out of which Rs. 2,500 was subsidy and the rest as loan. The P.O. had told that they can start business on this loan. But so far i.e. up to April 1987 the amount had not been given to the trained youths. A few trained boys were also contacted, who were satisfied with the training but could not utilise it.

For the year 1986-87, similar training for ten tribal youths was proposed to be arranged (under the Nucleus Budget) with the same Bandu Vanga Madavi as teacher. However upto April 1987 it was not started and neither Shri Madavi nor the local people reported about the starting of any such training class.

16. *Koyar*

Eleven kilometres to the south-east of Dhodraj is Koyar with nine houses and about 50 population.

This is also a village where the Chota Madia shifting cultivators were settled during 1959-60. Wild animals are often moving around this village as well as Murangal. At Koyar we came across a Madia of about 30-35 years age, well-built, who was attacked by a wild bear. His eye had been mutilated and he had several wounds on chest and back. Because he was intelligent enough, to lie down and imitate as if dead that the animal left him. Later the efforts of Dr. Prakash Amte at the Lok-Biradari Prakalpa at Hemalkasa saved his life.

In 1982-83 (under S.C.A.) a plantation plot of ground-nut was developed on two hectares of land as a demonstration plot. The Patel told that some ground-nut was taken away by the officer and rest was given to Madias. Though they liked it they did not grow it again for want of irrigation facilities.

There is only one well and the villagers demanded one tube-well.

Except one (Pusu Meena Pungati) all others got tiles for roofing.

Bullocks and carts were also given. The bullocks died in some cases.

Cows and she-goats are not given to any one and they want these benefits.

During 1982-83, under Special Central Assistance, a scheme of construction of Ghotul was implemented by the P.O. However, the traditional Ghotul was already present, only Mangalore tiles for roofing were given for the Ghotul under the so-called scheme of 'construction of Ghotul'.

17. *Kuvvakodi*

Kuvvakodi, consisting of Bada-Madia population has 24 houses (including 'tola') and population is around 150. Fifty-nine km away from Bhamragad, and 19 km ahead of Binagunda we reached Kuvvakodi after crossing big hills and a rough hilly terrain with steep slopes, through a thick bamboo forest. This is the last village on the Maharashtra border and, if we go down on the other side of the hill slopes we are in the Bastar area of Madhya Pradesh. It is from these hills that the Madias from this side go to M.P. for market at places like Jagdalpur etc.

The jeep can now go up, but even then atleast for half km one has to climb a small hill to enter the small village of 12 houses. The tola (annexe) is also of 12 houses. Perched at the centre of many big hills the village gives a photographic sight of huts with Banana, Papaiyya and other trees in the large courtyards. On the background are slopes of big hills, with patches of cut forest which is 'Penda' (shifting cultivation) still practised by Kuvvakodi people where they grow Kusari (a minor millet). Even on way to Kuvvakodi we could see families doing Kusari farming, on patches created by cutting forest which is called 'Penda'. It continues with the connivance of (or call it helplessness) forest officers.

Edma Banga Usendi, the Gayata of Kuvvakodi and its Tola is an old man of about 80-85 years age. He and his son Mura received us. The Gayata's term as Patel had expired and renewal was due. Shri E.Z. Khobragade the young energetic and dedicated S.D.O. of Aheri visited Kuvvakodi and signed an order 'on the spot' on 4-1-1987 (No. 2/x/87) renewing his term as Patel from 1-4-86 to 31-3-1991. The Gayata went to Bhamragad for his salary of the last one year on 20-3-87, but was not paid, (Kuvvakodi to Bhamragad is 59 km with an extremely difficult terrain, bad roads and no conveyance). The reason given by the Tahsildar was that the said order did not bear the seal of office. In fact a copy of the order was endorsed to him i.e. Tahsildar by the S.D.O. On way back I contacted Shri Khobragade, S.D.O. at Aheri and narrated the episode. He said that the D.S.P., Police Inspector and some revenue officers were with him and the order was signed in their presence and copy endorsed to the Tahsildar. The Tahsildar also knew all this. However he is unnecessarily delaying the payment. He also assured to look into the matter. By the time this report was finalised the needful was done by the S.D.O.

Tiles were given to seven houses including tola, and were given free to all.

Under a scheme under S.C.A. utensils were given to all families which included one big Brass-made water pot *(Handa)*, 2 alluminium utensils *(Ganjiya)*, 2 meal plates *(Thaliyan)*, 1 lid *(Dhakkan)*, 3 small bowls *(Katoriyan)*. One woollen blanket *(Ghongda)* was also given to all households. This was all given during 1986-87. These things were given without application (100% subsidy).

Pairs of bullocks were given in 1984-85 to eight beneficiaries. However not a single family was given bullock-cart. Probably it is difficult to reach the carts to the place and also there is a little scope to use it. i.e. to ride it on that road. But the villagers wanted carts and told that they can use these for farm work as well as for labour work.

A very typical scheme under N.B. (85-86) was that of giving expenses of marriage to Madia boys and girls. Around Rs. 450 were given to Mura Edma Usendi for his marriage with the girl viz. Kotla Masa Parsa of Binagunda.

Six persons – 4 girls and 2 boys participated in the trip to Nagpur organised by P.O. from N.B. The Binagunda boys and girls were also with them. They were happy with the trip and narrated experience.

Raju Soma Usendi and Kumma Shuku Usendi got Animal Husbandry training at Bhamragad in Feb. 1987 (1986-87) for one month with a stipend of Rs. 300 each and one cow, one calf and one Bull (for the village) were given to them. They also got milk-cans. They are selling milk to Paper Mill labour (there is a small camp of Bengali labour at the foot of the small hill over which Kuvvakodi is perched) @ Rs. 4 per litre. They (the Madia) also drink milk occasionally. (A change of great magnitude, because as per their tradition milking the cow and drinking milk is tabooed). They are also getting cycles in near future after depositing Rs. 130 per cycle.

There are Banana and Papaiyya trees in many courtyards and they told that they eat vegetable of raw fruit and also ripe fruits. This also is a change in food habits.

Under N.B. a scheme of construction of Ghotul was implemented during 1981-82 and 1982-83. Actually the Ghotul (roof) was fitted with galvanised tin sheets in 1986 though there was no such scheme during that year. This means that the scheme meant for 1981-82 and 1982-83 was implemented in 1986. We visited it with all villagers, including men, women, girls and the Gayata, saw the tin sheets fitted and later took group photographs.

In the houses along with traditional articles were also seen ladies, Brassiers, blouses, coloured clothes, ribbons, Mālās and many other articles were seen, indicating the impact of close contact with outside world (Bastar side) and a high level of acculturation as compared to the Madias, say, from Gundenhod, Aldandi, Bangadi, Bodange, Koyar etc.

The people are quite active, alert, fashionable – looking (the girls) though the married women still follow the tradition of putting only a waist cloth.

The village has no drinking water facility. They dig small holes and get water. This indicates that water is not much deep though the area is on hills at a height. The villagers demanded tube-well one each for the village and its Tola. They said the tube-well should be near the Ghotul.

They also demanded ploughing of their land by tractors. It is interesting to note that Penda (shifting cultivation) is still practised at Kuvvakodi which we observed. On way back a shifting cultivator (who was drunk) even blocked our road by putting a stem of a big tree cut from forest across the road and demanded two rupees as a price for taking photograph of his 'Kusari (cultivation i.e. Penda or shifting cultivation'.) Though they are shifting cultivators they demand ploughing by tractor which clearly shows that, shifting cultivation is now not so much, a part, of tradition but a 'duty under duress'. As, it is not possible for them to plough the land, 'Penda' is the only alternative. At the most it may be treated as 'a hobby' but not, strictly, tradition, or else, tractor ploughing would never have been accepted, leave apart demanded. This attitudinal change is worth noting both for anthropologists and administrators. It is now we i.e. the development administration which is falling short.

Apart from tiles for roofs, other things they want include money for labour, labour for bunding of farms, pairs of bullocks for all those families who don't possess it. After that they can grow paddy.

Presently they grow only minor millets – i.e. Kusari and cannot grow paddy.

On our way back, the smart young girls of Kuvvakodi with profuse tatooing on face and bright coloured clothes staged a *'Rasta Roko'* for us – blocked our way with a big bamboo in their hand – while we were negotiating a downward slope on foot. They wanted *'Bakshis'*. The old Gayata Edma, and old ladies with children on their lap were smiling and observing the childish blockade. It was really like a family affair. After I paid the '*bakshis*', we were reached up to our jeep which was standing near the foot of the hill. There was a case of burn injury to a small child. The wound was oozing and covered with flies etc. There were no chances of going to doctor so I opened my first-aid kit and gave cotton bundle, Burnol and demonstrated how to use the two items. With a promise to send copies of the photographs through the P.O. we left Kuvvakodi. It was refreshing experience in a remote corner and I saw a lot of understanding, eagerness, awareness, and better acculturation as compared to many other villages in the remote and secluded villages on the plains below.

If road communication is improved with regular Bus service between Allapalli to Kuvvakodi and ahead to Bastar, if their farms are ploughed and seeds given 'on time' and drinking water facilities and 'Bodis' supplied; if one dispensary and cultural-cum education centre established at Kuvvakodi, I am confident they will compete with their urban counterparts fairly well.

18. *Laheri*

Nineteen km from Bhamragad is Laheri a central village which is like a gate-way to the Bada Madia villages on hills. Since long, Laheri has had a mixed population with Madias, Gonds, Pardhans and Telis who have settled and become traders, *sahukars* and even local leaders. For many years the *Sarpanch* was a Teli. The new teacher-turned-leader Shri Malu Bogami- a Madia-Gond – who is an activist is also from Laheri. The Maharogi Seva Samiti of Warora which is running the Lok-Biradari Prakalpa at Hemalkasa is having one establishment at Laheri managed by Shri Mukund Dikshit. He runs a dispensary, a service centre catering to many minor needs of the tribals in the area and has created a mark in the area.

Being a big village situated on the main road many schemes were implemented by various departments.

Distribution of tiles for roof, pairs of bullocks and carts, training in Animal Husbandry with stipend of Rs. 300 followed by one cow and a calf, milk-cans, cycles etc. were the schemes implemented. Oil engines were given by T.D.O., the D.F.O. distributed earth-digging equipment *(Prakashtha Upakarns)* i.e. pan, spade, crow bar, pick-axe to tribal workers.

A cycle-shop was also granted to Shri Narango Pusu Naroti in 1984-85 who got four cycles and is running a cycle-Hire shop, charging 00.50 paise per hour. He said that spanners and other instruments were not given and hence repairs involve great expenditure.

A typical case was found regarding pair of bullocks and bullock-cart granted to Vatte Sonya Atram. He was granted pair of bullocks in 1984-85 and cart in 1985-86, but he has not received either of the things so far. To his surprise he has received a notice to pay loan instalment (the scheme being on 50 per cent subsidy the beneficiary has to pay half the cost as loan). He said he had not even signed (or put thumb impression) on any receipt of the benefits.

The three beneficiaries who got oil engines have developed very fine vegetable plantations and are growing ground-nut, onions, brinjals, chillies and one of them is also taking double crop. In April 1987 though summer had started his farm was green.

The beneficiaries who obtained cows after training are earning Rs. 4 per litre but the milk-yield had dwindled from 1-1/2 litres to one litre as grass is not available; they are feeding the cows with the dry stalks of paddy (*tanis*).

Solar tube lights are installed on road.

There is an Ashram School having classes from 1st to 7th standard (Primary and Middle class). There are 203 students. One Headmaster, seven teachers and one Balwadi Sevika form the staff. The Headmaster told that the I.Q. of Madia students is good and one student was admitted in Navodaya Vidyalaya at Ghot. The building is hut-like and the roof is also bad. The tin sheets fitted on the roof are very thin.

19. *Malampoddur*

Seven km from Dhodraj towards Laheri is Malampoddur, a big village, with population of 417; including Madia, Gonds, Pardhans, and Telis.

It has an Anganwadi and Kum. Nirmala Sitaram Sadmek is the Anganwadi worker. She was present and could be interviewed. This is the only village where we could find Anganwadi worker at Head-quarters. Thirty to thirty-five children come to Balwadi. The immunisation of children was not fully done and the medical staff did not turn-up to give the third dose of Triple antigen and Polio vaccine. She also reported that '*Sukhda*', (the protein rich food given,) is not always of good quality and once there were larvae worms in it. At times the children developed diarrhoea and stomach-ache after eating it. The Supervisor has not visited the Anganwadi during last one year and the C.D.P.O. (at Etapalli) has visited only once during the last three years. She has to go to Etapalli for collecting her monthly salary. T.A. Bills of the worker have not been paid even once during the last 3 years. The building for Anganwadi is under construction and she is temporarily holding it in a hut.

During 1981-82 under N.B.; dancers' troupes were provided with dresses etc. The material given to 5 boys and 5 girls who were dancers included sarees, blouses, shirts, ribbons, bangles, face-powder, combs, ear-rings, *ghungru* and such other decorative articles like beads necklaces etc.

In all, 13 persons got training in Animal Husbandry during 1986-87. A stipend @ Rs. 300 per head and one cow was given. Five of them also got Hero-make cycles in March 1987. Only Zuru Pedu Pallo did not receive the cow.

Roof-tiles have been given to twelve persons in 1984-85 and 1985-86. All of them got tiles.

Pairs of bullocks were distributed during 1984-85 and bullock-cart to one person in 1985-86.

One Bandu Masa Vadde is listed as a beneficiary under the scheme of 'repairs to hut'. He received tiles only for roofing.

20. *Murangal*

Five km from Dhodraj, to the S.E. is Murangal. It has 22 houses and the population is about 125.

During 1983-84 under N.B. a scheme for providing agricultural implements to Madia farmers ten persons got implements for earth-work like iron-pan, spade, crow-bar, pick-axe.

During 1982-83, under S.C.A. the P.O. gave Rs. 200 for levelling the land by putting earth, and the work was done by the local Madias and they got the amount towards labour done by them. Half hectare plot was levelled. While the records showed an outlay of Rs. 1,000 the villagers reported of having been paid Rs. 200 as labour charges for levelling under the scheme.

During 1982-83 only tiles were given for the Ghotul, under the scheme of 'construction of Ghotul' funded from S.C.A.

Seeds were given for sowing during 1983-84. During 1984-85 pairs of bullocks, carts etc. were also given to some of the villagers.

Recently a drain has been constructed on one side of the road in the village, but it is not used for draining water, but it may prove useful in rainy season.

Tugge Aara Pungati, Gayata of the village voiced the demands of the village and demanded pairs of bullocks, seed, tiles. On being reminded that as there is a Bodi, will he not ask for irrigation facility, he also added oil-engine to the list. His cart was of ordinary wood but as the bullocks died he could not use it. He said when the work of Paper Mill (i.e. BILT) is in progress, they earn by using carts and doing labour work for transporting bamboo.

21. *Nelgunda*

Seventeen km away from Dhodraj, on the south, is Nelgunda, which is at an extremity almost touching the border of the area.

Scheme of tiles for Ghotul was implemented here during 1983-84, however the tiles given were not sufficient as a result 1/4 the portion was covered with country tiles by the villagers (we could see this for ourselves).

A scheme of building '*Samaj Mandir*' (Community Centre) was also implemented in 1983-84 from S.C.A. and completed by 1986. The so-called 'Samaj Mandir' is an example as to what extent bungling in public works can go. There is a hall of about 13′ X 18′ with a varandah of 6′ X 18′. The construction is extremely bad, cracks have developed in walls and on floor and the cement floor is coming out with crests and troughs etc. The doors and windows are old, the wood has putrified and turned black and one can easily break the panels without much force. Very obviously these were brought from some old dilapilated house. It is a tiled structure and the roof is also very weak. This 'Samaj Mandir' building is worth visiting by any higher officer who wants to know why development does not take place in spite of huge funds being poured in tribal area by the Government. This Samaj Mandir exhibits 'the shameless faces of corruption'.

Another significant case was found in case of bullock-cart. Sayabi Dassa Varse got a bullock-cart, from Project Office and went to receive it. He signed the receipt and on inspection found that the cart had no iron tyres fitted on the wheels. The concerned officer told him to take it away and do whatever he can to do with it. Hence he met the Project Officer who asked him to see the clerk. The clerk told him to carry it, "as it is". Disgusted with this he did not take it with him though he had signed on the receipt register. Without iron tyres it was also not possible to carry that cart to Nelgunda, for which one has to cross a number of rivulets and *nullas* with black granite boulders and bad roads. It is surprising to note that instead of returning such an incomplete cart to the supplying agency the P.O. and his clerks persuaded the beneficiary to carry it in that form.

22. *Turremarka*

About six km from Binagunda on hills is Turremarka a Bada Madia village. Tin sheets were supplied to Ghotul during 1981-82, under the scheme of construction of Ghotul under S.C.A.

During 1982-83 thirteen beneficiaries got their houses built/ repaired on 100 per cent subsidy.

Kadba and *Kutar* was supplied to bullocks in 1981-82. This was reported to have been received by the beneficiaries.

During 1984-85 the T.D.C. supplied pairs of bullocks to five beneficiaries, some of the bullocks have died due to lack of doctor's visits.

One Badde Mura Podadi got Rs. 2,000 for purchase of goat and some villagers also got pigs.

Penda (shifting cultivation) still continues on the hills at Turremarka, they grow *kusari* and hence they call it '*Kusari* cultivation'.

I.T.D.P. Etapalli

1. *Chokhewada*

A village with 35 houses and 300 (approx.) population – about 95 per cent tribal (Madia-Gonds) population is situated between Kandhri and Todsa.

At Chokhewada two schemes implemented during 1985-86 were taken up for verification. The Panchayat Samiti (Etapalli) had sanctioned gobar-gas plants and five beneficiaries obtained the benefit. We visited the places of all the five beneficiaries and found that three beneficiaries viz. Yesu Danu Naroti, Rainu Madari Madavi and Nevru Gundru Gota were using the plant and used the gas for cooking purposes. They were even asked to switch on the gas-burners to see whether they really operate it or not. They did it well. However two beneficiaries viz. Rayaji Nanu Matami and Junglee Mahajan Usendi could not use it as their gas-plants were out of order. At Rayaji Nanu Matamis place, we observed that the Gobar-gas plant was of 'Janata' Model type and was constructed by a mason who was not skilled in constructing the plant. The levels of the tank and out-lets etc. were at defective levels, as a result gas could not come out. Due to this the whole thing had chocked. He could use it for 5-6 months but it was out of order from the last 3 months. The Panchayat Samiti officials did not bother to bring a skilled artisan to repair it. Only the Gram Sevak tried to help him but failed. The other plant also chocked.

Under the I.T.D.P. – Nucleus Budget, roofing tiles were given to five beneficiaries during 1985-86 (500 + 20 to each beneficiary). All had received the tiles and used them; which could be verified.

A typical scheme under the Nucleus Budget implemented during 1985-86 was Training in English typewriting. One Manku Ganu Matami (A student studying in B. Com. Part II class at Aheri and staying in Govt. Hostel) studied English typewriting at a private Typewriting Institute at Aheri for six months, and passed Typing Examination of 30 w.p.m. speed. Training fees @ Rs. 25 p.m. for six months and Rs. 40 Examination fees, were paid by the Project Office of the I.T.D.P. The total benefit amounted to Rs. 190. The student was satisfied with the training and hoped to get a job after passing his B. Com. final examination. He also said that the I.T.D.P. should help him for studying for post-graduation after passing the degree examination.

Shri Mangru Devu Naroti, the Perma (Bhagat) of Chokhewada and adjoining Madia villages is a social worker. He talked in an impressive manner and said that such a big village like Chokhewada had only one tube-well. He demanded atleast one more tube-well for the village.

2. *Dumme*

The Punjabrao Krishi Vidyapeeth has given a sewing machine to Patadi Pusu Pungati (a Madia) who is using it and earning livelihood as a support to agricultural income.

3. *Etapalli*

Etapalli is the headquarters of the Etapalli Tahsil, Etapalli Panchayat Samiti and of the I.T.D.P. – Gadchiroli No. I, the C.D.P.O.'s Office for the I.C.D.S. Etapalli area is also at Etapalli. It has a School (teaching up to S.S.C.) with Hostel and staff quarters. There is a TV set with a disc antenna, supposed to serve the school and the community around. There is a Primary Health Centre of the Zilla Parishad, a Post Office, State Bank of India Branch, Telephone Office, Forest Range office, Police Station and one Information Assistant of the M.S. Department of Information, Ballarpur Industries Pvt. Ltd. of Ballarpur is having their bamboo collection centre and a few officers posted at Etapalli. There is a rice-mill, grain and grocery shop; a few general, stainless-steel and cloth as well as readymade cloth stores, medical stores and one or two private doctors. The Punjabrao Krishi Vidyapeeth has a Tribal Area Research Unit at Aheri under a Research Scientist and they have adopted 8-10 villages around Etapalli for their research and extension work. They also give training in wood-work (carpentry), and give sewing machines to tribals etc.

Etapalli has a Forest Rest House and since 1986 a P.W.D. Rest House of the Government of Maharashtra has also been constructed. Etapalli is now well connected with Allapalli with a tar-top all season road. However, up to 1975-76 there was a road connecting Etapalli to Bhamragad directly through Burgi-Kandodi. Even State transport buses used to ply on this road during summer. For reasons unknown, this road was not only not converted in to a *pucca* road but there was no maintenance, as a result it went out of use. Now one has to return to Allapalli and take a circutous route to Bhamragad. This is strange because all the Head offices of Development Departments are at Etapalli and there is (at least ought to be) easy communication between the staff at Bhamragad and ahead up to Kuvvakodi and their headquarters. at Etapalli. I was informed that the same old road is now to be taken-up for repairs (after 8-10-years of lapse).

The TV Set with a dish antenna at the Zilla Parishad School, Etapalli is just a show-piece. It is under the control of Headmaster. It worked for 2-3 months and now for the last 3 years or more it is lying unused. Some minor fault in the antenna unit has hampered its use for the community. However neither the Headmaster has any powers to get it repaired nor is there any other provision for repairs and maintenance. A research team reported that though the Government claimed 100 per cent coverage of the Gadchiroli district under television, they found in their survey that only four sets are working in the district others went out of order during the first 2-4 months after installation.

The Project Officer of Etapalli implemented a scheme of distribution of bicycles (from N.B.) to school children from Etapalli Zilla Parishad School. When I insisted for getting an authentic list of beneficiaries the Zilla Parishad school office told that the list and other relevant papers were not traceable. The new Headmaster could not succeed in persuading the clerk to find it out. However, in Etapalli there is a talk that many others e.g., teachers, etc. took advantage of the scheme and took away the cycles, which on record were issued to the school children. Due to the non-availability of the list of beneficiaries from the school the facts could not be verified.

It is worth mentioning that Etapalli has been sanctioned a country-wine shop under licence from the Govt. of Maharashtra. As per law such shops are not allowed in such tribal areas. The reason given was that Etapalli has a good percentage of non-tribal population and hence it was allowed. The non-tribals at Etapalli are mostly office staff of the State Govt. offices. So! what does this mean? Is it a provision for them? We must also note that within distance ranging from 2 km to 20 km there are many Madia villages with 90-100 per cent tribal population who also daily visit Etapalli. They are also served at this shop. All this shows how we follow the law in words (to suit some-one's(?) interests) and evade the spirit of the laws, skipping over even the 'pious' policies of tribal development.

4. *Geda*

At village Geda one Danu Katiya Pada (a Madia) got electric pump for irrigation from T.D.O. The Gram Sevak told him and helped him to apply. But since last one year the pump is unused as the electric wire of the main line is broken. Even after several requests the line-man is not repairing it and demands Rs. 250 for the same. The pump also needs repairs. Thus though the pump can be very useful he is unable to use it.

5. *Jarawandi*

About 40 km away from Etapalli is village Jarawandi with about 80 houses. Seven beneficiaries under different schemes were covered.

The schemes included loans for starting shops (General stores, Grocery, Vegetables etc.) from the M.S. Tribal Development Corporation, Goat-keeping and sewing machines etc.

It was interesting to observe that out of four beneficiaries to whom loans for starting shops were sanctioned none had actually started it.

Shri Laxman Mahadeo Kodape was sanctioned a loan of Rs. 5,000 (1985-86) for starting a General Stores. There was no such 'Store'. However he was already running a *Pan*-shop (*Pan Thela* – i.e. a shed on quadrupod wooden stand) and the people reported that he had kept some articles for sale in the same Pan-Thela. Since some days, he was out of station and hence could not be interviewed.

Shri Harischandra Lahuji Madavi was another beneficiary to whom a loan of Rs. 5,000 for starting a General Stores was sanctioned in 1985-86. He started a Store at *Kasansur* and *not* at Jarawandi.

Shri Prabhakar Saoji Meshram was sanctioned a loan of Rs. 2,000 for starting a '*Maneri* shop' (*Maneri* usually consists of bangles, articles made of beads, cosmetics, ribbons etc.). He was working as a peon in an office at village Rangi and had not started a *Maneri* shop.

The fourth shop was sanctioned to Shri Bisan Arjun Madavi staying at village Kandhri (near Jarawandi) for starting a vegetable shop (*Bhajipala* – *Sabji* shop) at Jarawandi. This was sanctioned before 7-8 months but he had not actually started the shop. On contacting the Manager of T.D.C. at Kasunsur it was known that Shri Madavi had received the 1st instalment of loan (Rs. 500 i.e. 50% of the total amount) but had not started the shop.

Shri Bhanudas Zingruji Madavi was sanctioned Rs. 2,000 for purchasing goats. His name is displayed in the list on notice-board at Etapalli office of the M.S.T.D. Corporation but he had not received any written intimation and hence had not gone to collect the loan.

Two cases of beneficiaries who got loans for sewing machines were interesting – Smt. Jamunabai Dattu Madavi and Shri Namdeo Subhan Madavi obtained Rs. 1,500 each for purchase of sewing machines. Both of them have purchased machines and are getting good business as tailors. Both beneficiaries were satisfied and felt that they could support their families and progress due to the benefit.

6. *Javelli*

The gobar-gas plant scheme was implemented by Panchayat Samiti at Javelli. During 1983-84 and 1984-85 the two beneficiaries were Girma Sitaram Meshram and Bichanga Durga Talandi. In the first case i.e. Girma Sitaram Meshram, the plant was thrust upon him (probably to show work) though *he had no cattle heads to feed gobar to the plant*. Consequently, since construction, it is unused. In the case of Bichanga Talandi also, the plant is out of order since beginning as the gas never came out. He also does not know how to operate it. The Panchayat Samiti officials never enquired or tried to put it in to operation though Javelli is hardly 10 km away from Panchayat Samiti headquarters i.e. Etapalli.

Sewing machines were given by the Tribal Area Research Project of the Punjabrao Krishi Vidyapeeth field unit at Aheri to Namdeo Musli Atram and Bajirao Some Sidam. Both of them are using them and earning livelihood on tailoring.

7. *Kandhali*

During 1985-86, Shri Bisan Arjunji Madavi who was sanctioned Rs. 1,000 for starting a *Sabji* shop (Vegetable shop) had received Rs. 500 from the M.S.T.D. Corporation, seven to eight months back but had not opened a shop. He said he will open it at Jarawandi.

During 1985-86 five beneficiaries were given tiles for roofing (600+30) under the I.T.D.P. All of them reported that they obtained tiles and we could see the tiled roofs.

8. *Kasansur*

About 60 km away from Etapalli, Kasansur is linked with a good, all season road. A village with 62 houses it has a good infrastructure including the following:

(i) Ashram School – with a good building and campus.
(ii) Anganwadi Centre (under I.C.D.S.)
(iii) Community Recreation Centre.
(iv) Primary Health Centre.

(v) Branch Post-office.
(vi) Visit and Training Centre under the Benor-scheme of the Agriculture Department.
(vii) Gramin Bank (attached to Lead Bank).
(viii) Forest Range-office.
(ix) The Horticultural Plantation Farm of Gadchiroli district.

The schemes studied were gobar-gas plants, oil engines and poultry farming.

The Tribal Development Officer, Aheri had sanctioned oil engines to Shri Komti Devu Madavi (1978-79), Shri Dasru pati Hedo (1980-81) and Raju Dolu Narotey (1984-85). All the three oil engines are in good condition and all the three beneficiaries reported increase in production and in their incomes. We also visited and saw them functioning.

The M.S.T.D. Corporation sanctioned loan of Rs. 5,000 for starting a General Store (1985-86) to Shri Kotla Malu Pallo but he has not collected the amount as he was scared by others. (Others telling him that it will be difficult to earn profits and pay back loans etc.).

The T.D.C. also sanctioned Rs. 2,000 to Manu Chaitu Pallo for Poultry farming (1985-86) but he also did not collect the amount.

The Panchayat Samiti sanctioned two Gobar-gas (their list states 'Bio-gas' but actually it is Gobar gas) plants. Both are not in working order. Shri Dasru Pati Helo's plant is all choked-up and he could not get any benefit out of it. Neither the Panchayat Samiti officials nor the Gobar-gas expert of the Village Industries office turned up to check it.

9. *Krishnar*

About five kilometres away from Etapalli is village Krishnar with 99 per cent Madia population. With 30 houses and 245 population it has a creche-centre run by an all India organisation – the Bharatiya Adimjati Sevak Sangh (BAJSS), New Delhi. The field headquarters of the BAJSS is located at Krishnar in a tiled hut and they have a community centre in a Madia style Ghotul. The life-worker of the BAJSS stays there with his wife and family and has given lead to awareness and developmental activities including five creches and two balwadis.

New crops have been introduced by the BAJSS worker and the Madias have adopted many of the new crops. A voluntary organisation 'Navrang Mandal' of local Madia youths has been formed under the life-workers guidance, which is exclusively managed by Madias and organised Kabaddi, Volley ball and other tournaments in the area.

The Tribal Research and Development Council, a voluntary organisation and the Continuing Education and Extension Department of the Nagpur University had also collaborated with the BAJSS and organised their own programmes in and around village Krishnar. The various programmes organised periodically include tree plantation, prohibition awareness and population education programmes. Also organised are training camps for tribal youths in Kabaddi and Volleyball, annual tournaments for Madia Youths from the Etapalli Panchayat Samiti area in Kabaddi and Volley-ball and annual dancing competitions of Madias in their traditional dances.

However very few schemes under the ITDP were operated in village Krishnar.

There are three Gobar-gas plants in the village out of which none is functioning. It is choked-up for the last many years.

Two Madias got oil-engines and both are functioning. Firangi Peka Kando, a Madia farmer who has one, reported that repairing it was a problem. The other beneficiary Ganda Hichami also reported, they don't get diesel and have to go 35 km to Allapali where there is only one petrol-pump which also never has sufficient stock of diesel.

Electric poles were erected and line was laid through Krishnar, Marpalli and other surrounding villages but the line was not charged for two and a half years. On enquiry the concerned officers of M.S.E.B. reported that the line was to be connected to the supply line for which cutting of some forest trees was essential. The Forest Department did not allow and the papers had to be sent to New Delhi as per their new forest policy. Consequently the whole expenditure on laying the line was a waste for 2-3 years. Recently line is charged and street lights are provided.

10. *Pandhevahi*

Ghisu Irpa Atram was persuaded to get a Gobar-gas plant constructed at his place though he did not want it. The Village Development Officer of Panchayat Samiti persuaded him. However the plant is out of order.

II

EVALUATION OF THE BENEFITS — SCHEME-WISE

A. Individual Beneficiary Schemes

In the Bhamragad I.T.D.P. (Primitive tribes) area out of the total individual beneficiary schemes (meaning that the benefit was for an individual) studied the maladies were as under:

1. *Scheme for giving Pairs of Bullocks/Bullock-carts/Carts*

Out of 33 beneficiaries to whom pairs of bullocks were reported to have been given, only one complained of not having received the benefit.

Out of 15 beneficiaries to whom bullocks and carts were granted one has not received the benefit though a notice for repayment of loan has been received by him.

Out of 14 beneficiaries to whom cart was granted 5 irregular cases were found. In two cases the beneficiaries signed receipt but did not bring it and in one of the two cases the wheels of cart had no iron tyres and even after complaining to the P.O. he was told to take it away 'as it Is'. Consequently he did not bring it. In yet another case the beneficiary refused to take delivery of the cart (from Forest Department) as the wood was of bad quality. In the fifth case the cart was delivered in the next year when the beneficiary had died and hence his son received the cart.

2. *Tiles for Roofing of Huts* (400 + 30 Manglore tiles)

Out of 49 beneficiaries 22 cases of irregularity were found out: In two cases the tiles were taken by another person than the beneficiary and in one case it was reported that with a couple of showers of rain the tiles dissolved. People from villages Hiddur, Kiyar and Hitapadi reported that they were asked to get operated for family planning as a condition for getting tiles. There were 15 such cases at Hiddur where they personally narrated this to us. One man even told that even after F.P. operation he did not get tiles. At Kiyar four persons including a woman reported the same thing. At Hitapadi also two beneficiaries reported that they got tiles only after F.P. operation and one reported that even after his operation he was not given tiles.

3. *Repair to Hut*

Out of the total three beneficiaries all the three reported that they got tiles for roofs of their huts and that was the only 'repair' – work done. This appears to be the same scheme of 'Tiles for roofing' under a different name.

4. *Broom Purchase*

Only one case was reported in the lists provided. Actually this was a scheme for preparation and sale of brooms by tribals. However the female beneficiary reported that she never applied nor does she want any such assistance.

5. *Brick-making*

One beneficiary was granted loan but such a brick-making unit was not started.

6. *Shops*

Cycle-hire (Taxi) shops were granted to two beneficiaries and they started the shop and were getting good income. They wanted spanners etc. for maintenance of cycles.

The grocery shop and vegetable shop granted were not started at all.

7. *Oil Engines*

Out of nine beneficiaries who got the oil engines, one had given it on hire to others and the other could not show it, probably he had also given it to some-one. Thus two such irregular cases were found. However in the other seven cases where the beneficiaries were using the benefit some complaints/shortcomings of the scheme included:

(a) Non-availability of diesel and thus extortion by other Departments staff for supplying diesel.
(b) Spanners, pipe/tube not given.

(c) Problem of maintenance/repairs.

The Etapalli I.T.D.P. Area

1. *Electric Pump*

In the Etapalli I.T.D.P. area the scheme of electric-motor pumps was operated. The only (one) pump given to a beneficiary who was studied, was not in use due to fault in the electric supply line. (Please see the statement supplied by the T.D.O. showing the position of electric pumps (see Table 5.3).

Tribal Development Officer, Aheri, (Distt. Gandhiroli)

TABLE 5.2: Information Regarding Oil-engine Pumps

Sl. No.	Year in which pump sanctioned	Total Number of pumps sanctioned farmers	Pumps actually delivered to	Remarks
1.	1978-79	6	6	The Maharashtra State Tribal Development Corporation informed that the pumps for 1985-86 will be supplied at the earliest
2.	1979-80	8	8	
3.	1980-81	24	24	
4.	1981-82	19	19	
5.	1982-83	14	14	
6.	1983 84	7	7	
7.	1984-85	25	25	
8.	1985-86	19	—	
	Total	122	103	

2.*Gobar-gas Plants*

Operated by the Panchayat Samiti, out of 13 plants eight were out of order due to choking. Only six were in good condition. In one case the beneficiary had no cattle and hence told that he did not want the plant but it was thrust upon him. It is unused since installation. In these cases of failure the Panchayat Samiti officers first persuaded the tribals to accept the scheme but later neither supervised over construction nor the maintenance, Some are wrongly constructed (the 'Janata' plants) and except a stray case the Gram Sevak also does not take interest.

Tribal Development Officer, Aheri (Distt. Gadchiroli).

TABLE 5.3: Information Regarding Electric Motor Pumps

Sl. No.	Sanction Year	Sanctioned number of pumps	No. of pumps actually installed	Pumps not installed	Pumps in use after electric supply	Pumps not yet functioning	Pumps presently in use	Pumps not in use	Remarks
1.	1973-74	9	9	—	9	—	—	9	Pump out of order/Non-payment of bill.
2.	1974-75	2	2	—	2	—	—	2	Pump out of order/Non-payment of bill.
3.	1975-76	3	2	1	2	—	1	1	Non payment of bill.
4.	1976-77	1	1	—	1	—	1	—	Pump out of order/Non payment of bill,
5.	1977-78	7	7	—	7	—	—	7	Pump out of order/Non payment of bill.
6.	1978-79	12	12	—	12	—	4	8	Pump out of order/Non payment of bill.
7.	1979-80	12	11	1	11	—	3	8	Pump out of order/Non payment of bill.
8.	1980-81	11	10	1	8	2	2	8	Pump out of order/no electric connection
9.	1981-82	4	4	—	4	—	1	3	Pump out of order/no electric connection
10.	1982-83	5	5	—	4	1	2	3	Pump out of order/no electric connection
11.	1983-84	7	7	—	3	4	2	5	No electric supply from M.S.E.B.
12.	1984-85	7	7	—	—	7	—	7	Non receipt of T.R. from T.D.C.
13.	1985-86	12	—	—	—	—	—	—	Pump not supplied by T.D.C.
	Total	92	77	3	63	14	16	61	

Tribal Development Officer Aheri (Distt. Gadchiroli).

TABLE 5.4: Action taken of Applications Received for Oil-pumps and Electric Pumps during 1986-87

Sl. No.	Scheme	Total No. of Appli	Well	Nulla	River	Sent to the concerned Deptt. for feasibility certificate		Feasibility-certified applications		Non-feasibility		Remarks
						MSEB	GSDA	MSEB	GSDA	MSEB	GSDA	
1.	Supply of electric pumps to tribal farmers on 100 per cent subsidy	20	15	5	—	20	15	8	—	—	—	Incomplete applications are being completed by meeting farmers or by post.
2.	Supply of oil pumps to tribal farmers on 100 per cent subsidy	41	24	14	3	36	21	—	—	—	—	3 Applications are not eligible
	Total	61	39	19	3	56	36	8	—	—	—	

Tribal Development Officer, Aheri, (Distt. Gadchiroli)

TABLE 5.5: Supply of Electric/Oil Pumps under 20-Point Programme during 1986-87

Sl. No.	Scheme	Target given	Provision in Lakhs (Rs.)	Expenditure incurred (Rs.)	Remarks
1.	Electric Pumps on 100 per cent subsidy to tribal farmers	12	1.10	2,240.00	–
2.	Oil pumps on 100 per cent subsidy to tribal farmers	14	1.40	–	–
3.	Special Central Assistance for (Electric pumps)	–	1.00	–	–
4.	Special Central Assistance (Oil pumps)	–	0.10	–	–

Note: 1. For the year 1986-87 20 applications for electric pumps and 28 for Oil engines have been received.

3. *Agricultural Inputs*

Fertilisers and other agricultural inputs were supplied through Panchayat Samiti. The farmers never received these things in time and hence the benefit was not much useful to them. Though the scheme is good it is not properly implemented. During the last sowing season non-official workers (activists) are reported to have distributed paddy in Bhamragad area out of the funds collected by them from contractors etc.

4. *General Stores/Maneri Shop/Vegetable Shop*

Out of the three general stores financed by M.S.T.D.C., one beneficiary did not collect the amount, the other just kept articles in his *Pan*-shop (*Thela*) and the third one started it at another place. The *Maneri* shop granted to one beneficiary is not started.

A *Maneri* shop was granted, however the beneficiary did not start it though he received half the sanctioned amount.

One beneficiary received half the amount for vegetable shop but did not start it.

5. *Goat-keeping/Poultry*

In the two cases — studied one each per scheme — the benefit was granted but the beneficiaries under both the schemes did not collect the amount.

B. The Group — Beneficiary Schemes

Under these schemes the beneficiary was a group/community/ organisation etc. who received the benefit and through them it reached the individual(s).

1. *Group of Different Schemes granted to the Lok-Biradari Prakalpa at Hemalkasa*

The Lok-Biradari Prakalpa at Hemalkasa, run by the Maharogi Seva Samiti, a public trust with its headquarters at Warora is the only and major recipient of group benefits. From the discussions and study (Please see village-wise evaluation of beneficiaries) it is obvious that it is the Project Officer who took initiative in preparing schemes for the L.B.P. obviously because it was easy, convenient and more-fool proof for him. The L.B.P. is working at Hemalkasa since 1975 and has done pioneering work in the sphere of health services to tribals and primary education and also in increasing the levels of awareness and functionality in the area.

As reported earlier, the amount for medicines used to be granted at the end of the financial year, however on the suggestion of the L.B.P. it was streamlined and the requirements of medicines and medical equipment is now given throughout the year as per needs of tribal/patients who came to L.B.P. Hospital.

The amount spent on uniforms of children sounds too high considering the wholesale purchase of uniforms (or of cloth and tailoring charges).

The important aspect in these schemes is that the services envisaged under the schemes by utilising the amount did — in fact — reach the tribals.

2. *Spread of Fish-Seed in Lakes/Two Ferry Boats at Bhamragad*

The Fishermens' Cooperative Society at Bhamragad had organised training for fishermen. It was to this Society that the fish-seed was given. The President of the Society, Dunga Irpa Gumma was telling that the lake gave good fish-crop. This very society was also to use the two ferry-boats for catching fish in the big rivers (Indravati, Perlakuta, Nibra or Pamal Gautam) on the nexus of which the village is situated. A few members of the society who were present also expressed satisfaction over the fish production.

Ferry-boats can be regularly used for reaching nearby villages on the other side of the nexus of rivers, like Gollaguda etc. circumventing a long distance of say 10-15 km.

3. *Demonstration Plots in Vegetables and Horticulture*

The scheme was implemented during 1981-82, 1982-83 and 1985-86 and such plots developed at Binagunda, Koyar etc. Extension workers throughout the world agree that result demonstration is one of the best methods of extension. Here also this has been proved. In addition, the Forest Department and the Ballarpur Industries Ltd., Ballarpur have also taken up this scheme. At Gundenhod the B.I.L.T. has developed such a plot. The demonstration plot at Binagunda is presently (1986-87) developed by the Forest Department. The Department is also sowing paddy and distributing it. Fruit trees, ground-nut, vegetable gardens are now seen at Laheri, Kuvvakodi and some other villages which is a result of these demonstration plots.

What is now required is a follow-up by providing irrigation facility and other pre-requisites so that those willing can grow such plots. Quick marketing facilities and fruit-preservation courses and facilities may also be provided.

4. *Construction of Community Centres (Samaj Mandirs)*

This scheme was implemented during 1983-84 and 1984-85. This was taken up under Special Central Assistance. The Madia-Gonds have a traditional Community Centre for youths called 'Ghotul'. However, it is interesting to note that there was another scheme called 'Construction of Ghotul'. The Samaj Mandirs' construction at three places present a sad picture. The one at 'Nelgunda' is the worst (Please see details under village-wise evaluation). The one at Dh[illegible]aj is relatively better but that too represents a worn out and cracked (though new) structure. Moreover, since construction, there is no use to 'Samaj' but State Reserve Police personnel are camping, in it. At Gundenhod there is no 'Samaj Mandir', but roofing tiles are given to the Ghotul which was already there.

5. *Repairs to Ghotul*

This scheme was just giving tiles for the Ghotul roof. Only at Kuvvakodi galvanised tin-sheets have been given. In fact this scheme can be properly implemented with participation of the local community. At village Krishnar the BAJSS has constructed a complex consisting of worker's quarters and Ghotul (there was no Ghotul at Krishnar) at a meagre cost of Rs. 4,000 only. Considering the community spirit and their interest in Ghotuls, the Department should use the people's participation and shramadan method for such scheme.

The Gaita of Binagunda, among other things wanted expansion and repairs of the Ghotul. The Project Officer told me that he very often visits Binagunda and stays in the Ghotul. I asked the Gaita whether he had not brought this demand to the notice of the P.O. He did not give any specific answer.

6. *Madia-Shibir*

Two training camps for Madias were held during 1983-84 under S.C.A. out of the proposed three camps. These two camps were held at Binagunda and Bhamragad respectively. The Binagunda people reported that a health camp — diagnostic type — was held during that year. The title of the scheme does not indicate the nature and purpose of the camps.

7. *Study Trip of Madias to Different Places*

Trips were organised to places like Bombay, Nagpur, Chandrapur, Warora etc. The youths and girls who went with the tour were very happy with the experience. They narrated of having seen poultry farms, zoo, aeroplanes, railway trains, buses, hotels, schools and colleges and persons like Baba Amte. The level of awareness, understanding and alertness was obviously raised.

8. *C.D. Works*

The scheme of cross drainage implemented through the P.W. Department consisted of small bridges on *kuccha* forest roads so that water-logging on the roads during rainy season could be avoided. About Rs. 4 lakhs have been spent up to 1984 from S.C.A. However, the work done is absolutely useless. We could negotiate easily through the rest of the road but wherever C.D. Work was done our Jeep had to take a diversion. Big boulders perched in knee-deep dust over pieces of pipe — all in an haphazard manner — was the show. God only knows what will happen to the work during rains. It was just spoiling the roads.

9. *Construction of Administrative Complex at Bhamragad for Project Office and Staff Quarters*

This scheme was taken under S.C.A. funds and up to 1984 Rs. 9,52,000 were spent on it. Rs. 7 lakhs were again spent during 1985-86 on project staff quarters. The complex consisting of the Project Office and staff quarters consists nearly of seven units. The quarters including that of the Project Officer was having roofs of Mangalore tiles. The wood used for doors and windows is not of teak (the whole area is full of best teak-wood forest — Allapalli teak boasts of being one of the best in the World and during the years these buildings were constructed teak was being sold in cities like Chandrapur at the *retail rate of* about Rs. 125 per cubic foot) and they used other lower quality wood which is sold at a still lower rate. On the whole the quality of construction is bad and they could have been built for a much lesser amount. A new unit is under construction.

10. *Distribution of Uniforms to Children*

Uniforms to children from Anganwadis, Balwadis and schools were distributed. This scheme was operated through Lok-Biradari and directly by the Project Officer. On verification the parents from all the villages reported of having received the uniforms. The cloth used was fair, but considering that these must have been purchased/ stitched on a large scale the cost sounds to be too high. Similarly Table 5.6 shows the glaring disparity of the cost of uniforms distributed.

TABLE 5.6: Statement showing Expenditure on Distribution of Uniforms to School Children and Average Per Uniform Expenditure

The scheme operated by	Year	Amount Spent	No. of students	Student-uniform Expenditure
Lok-	1982-83 (N.B.)	25,000	216	115.74
Biradari	1984-85 (N.B.)	25,000	250	100.00
Prakalpa	1985-86 (N.B.)	24,800	250	99.20
Hemalkasa	1986-87 (N.B.)	24,948	275	90.72
Project	1983-84 (S.C.A.)	47,976	1500	31.98
Officer	1985-86 (N.B.)	24,800	1240	20.00
	1986-87 (N.B.)	24,920	280	89.00

11. *Dancing Equipment to Madia Dancers*

Dancers from ten Madia villages were given dancing equipment which included blouses, sarees (usually Madia girls, women don't use these — hence covered under 'equipment'), *Ghungru*, ribbons, *gondas,* powder, earrings, bangles etc. These were reported to have been received by the dancers.

12. *Training in Crafts to Madia Tribals*

Training in metal craft and wood craft was reported to have been arranged in 1982-83 at Kiyar and Laheri respectively and metal craft training proposed in 1986-87 had not been arranged up to April 1987. The trainees of the previous training were satisfied with training but could not get follow-up facilities for starting the business which was promised to them by the Project Officer.

13. *Training to Madia Teachers in Madia Dialect**

The State Institute of Educational Research and Training organises, through the collaboration of Zilla Parishad, a training course in Madia dialect, of a weeks duration for primary school teachers teaching in the area. The teachers working in the area told that they were benefited by the course and one teacher who had undergone this training and who accompanied us to some villages could converse very well in Madia dialect with villagers.

14. *Solar-Tube Lights**

These are fitted on streets at Bhamragad, Arewada, Laheri, etc. and give good light up to 4-5 A.M. However, the remote villages are not given these light. It is more in the nature of a show business. In fact these should first be fitted in villages like Aldandi, Bangadi, Koyar, Murangal etc. Each unit costs Rs. 25,000. There is no provision for repairs and maintenance.

15. *Ashram Schools*

Operated by the Tribal Development Officer at Aheri, there are in all five Ashram Schools, one each at Kasansur, Todsa, Jambia, Laheri and Jarawandi. Thus, the only Ashram School under the I.T.D.P. (Primitive Tribes) Bhamragad is at Laheri and was started in 1976-77. It has classes from 1st to 7th standard i.e. Primary and Middle school levels. In 1986-87 session there were 203 students (as per the figure displayed in Headmaster's office — the statistics supplied by T.D.O. shows 260). There are seven teachers and one Balsevika for the Balwadi attached to it. In the first standard, children are taught through Madia-Gondi — their mother-tongue and later Marathi is introduced.

Students from 5-7 km distance are admitted. Lodging, boarding, bedding, two uniforms, books, exercise-books, writing material etc. are supplied free of cost. School is in small building of Zilla Parishad. Two temporary shades on the aid given by Maharashtra. Small Industries Corporation are used for the girl students. The campus of the school is very small.

The concept of Ashram School Complex envisaged in the original blue-print of the Tribal Sub-plan is not put to practice.

The Ashram Schools at Kasansur and Todsa (under I.T.D.P. — Etapalli) are relatively better and the one at Kasansur has a very good building, play ground and other facilities.

---

* These two are non-T.S.P. schemes, however are covered as they support the process of development in the area.

The Integrated Child Development Scheme

The C.D.P.O. i.e. Child Development Project Officer of the Integrated Child Development Services Scheme (I.C.D.S.) outlined the organisation of the Department. Hundred per cent expenditure on this scheme is incurred by the Government of India, under its Minimum Needs Programmes. However the Central Government gives these funds to the Maharashtra State Government which operates the scheme. Up to 31st March, 1984 this scheme was managed by the Rural Development Department through the Zilla Parishad as a transferred scheme and as such the Chief Executive Officer of the Zilla Parishad was the Chief at the District level. Since 1st April, 1984, a Directorate has been created at the State Level with Headquarters at Nasik. At the district level one District Programme Officer has been appointed, with H.Qs. at Gadchiroli. At the Panchayat Samiti Level the Child Development Project Officer is the Chief, which is a class I post. They are non-technical officers with two months orientation training in the subject-matter.

Under the C.D.P.O. there is the following staff. There are three Supervisors (always ladies, called 'Mukhya Sevikas') who are also non-technical, who have received two months training at Kosbad. Below these supervisors there are Anganwadi Workers, one worker managing one centre. They also receive three months training. Each worker has an helper to help her in managing the centre.

Under the C.D.P.O. there is also a technical team with one Medical Officer (who should be an M.B.B.S. Doctor). Under him there are two Health Visitors (who are supervisors) and under them there are four Auxiliary Nurse-cum-Midwives (ANM). However in Etapalli Panchayat Samiti area all these posts are lying vacant.

At the Panchayat Samiti level there is a Co-ordination Committee of three officers viz., the Project-cum-Block Development Officer, C.D.P.O. and Medical Officer of the Primary Health Centre.

There is one Jeep and twelve Luna Moped Vehicles available for the unit.

Envisaged Objectives of the I.C.D.S.

The purpose of the whole scheme is that the people and particularly women must know the importance of nutritious food and should nurse their Children accordingly. In the Etapalli Panchayat Samiti area there are fifty Anganwadi Centres. Each Anganwadi worker is supposed to look after the children who assemble at the centre. They are taught like Balwadi students but the emphasis is more on cleanliness and discipline. In the Etapalli Panchayat Samiti area there are 312 villages. As per Government norms there ought to be one centre for 100 population, but, for this area it has been brought to 700. The C.D.P.O. has recommended that there should be one centre for 300 population considering the problems and typical conditions in the area. There are twenty-seven centres in Etapalli area, six in Bhamragad area and seventeen spreadover in the remaining area. The C.D.P.O. has demanded 75 additional centres for effectively covering all the areas. Since 1985 fifty-one are sanctioned and are supposed to have started.

Children between the age group 3–6 are served at the Anganwadi Centre. They are given Polio doses, B.C.G. and triple antigen (D.P.D.) vaccines and injections. The Medical side is considered very important and care of every child is taken. Nutritional diet is distributed free of cost on every alternate day. In case of children who are below the standard 'age-height-weight' ratio, double nutrition is given. Normally milk/powder milk is given under this scheme but in this area the Madia tribals are against drinking milk and hence that is not given. Ground-nut seeds and Gram (*Chana*) is soaked in water and distributed after roasting or frying it in oil with some salt and chillies. Jaggery (*Gur*) is also distributed.

A special food called '*Sukli*' (or *sukhda*) was also distributed in some areas, which has flour of Bulger, Soyabean powder and oil with Jaggery. It was roasted and supplied in packets by Shri Sadguru Seva Sangh for some time. The first three ingredients in this diet were supplied by C.A.R.E. under sane agreement. This food could get good response from tribals but later on the quality of the food declined. At present it is not being distributed in Etapalli Panchayat Samiti area.

The I.C.D.S. Experience

These centres also take care of pregnant and feeding mothers. They are given medical aid and efforts are made to create awareness about nutrition and nutritious diets. They are supposed to be educated accordingly. However as stated by the C.D.P.O. this objective has not been fully achieved. Their food habits could not be changed. One of the reasons given by the C.D.P.O. for the inadequacy of the machinery, was, that local girls were not available for working as Anganwadi workers, ladies are orthodox and superstitious in their beliefs, and as such give poor adoption of all the new items of nutrition, child care etc. canvassed by them. Hence the efforts to educate them, have failed.

However the C.D.P.O. said that the vaccines and inoculations are popularised in the sense that the women bring their children to these centres and don't resist when these immunisation programmes are held.

In the Etapalli I.C.D.S. which covers the whole Etapalli Panchayat Samiti area, there were originally fifty Anganwadis, fifty-one were added bringing the total to 101. In the Bhamragad I.T.D.P. area, out of the villages studied nine villages are shown to have Anganwadi Centres as per list. These villages include Bhamragad, Dhodraj, Malampaddur and Arewada in the first fifty, while in the additional centres are included Aldandi, Nelgunda, Gongwada, and Binagunda.

In the Etapalli I.T.D.P. area among the villages studied Anganwadis are at Etapalli, Javelli, Dumme, Pandhewadhi, Chokhewada.

Evaluation

In the Bhamragad area we did not come across Anganwadi at Aldandi, Nelgunda, Gongwada and Binagunda. At Bhamragad, Dhodraj and Malampoddur there were Anganwadis but the Anganwadi worker was found at H.Qs. only at Bhamragad and at Malampoddur. The Aldandi People demanded an Anganwadi at that place.

The average attendance of children at these Anganwadis was 30 — 35. The Madia parents are sending children to Anganwadis. House visits for advising pregnant women are also undertaken. The immunisation programme also exists. However a Anganwadi worker reported, that the programme is not properly implemented and supervised.

The shortcomings pointed out included the following:

(i) Polio vaccine and Triple antigen were given but after 2 doses, dose was not repeated.

(ii) The nutritious food given usually included '*Sukhda*'. At times worms/larvae were found in it, however the same was distributed to children.

(iii) The Supervisor has not paid a single visit to the area/village during the last one year.

(iv) The C.D.P.O. has paid a single visit to the area during the last three years.

(v) There are no good rooms for the Anganwadis, and whenever they are built they are given/occupied by other Government Officers etc. and at places by the S.R.P. personnel.

The Project Officer has distributed uniforms to Anganwadi children under the schemes already studied.

In the Etapalli area also some of the Anganwadis are not working.

The BAJSS, New Delhi is already running a creche at Krishnar for the last 5-6 years and one more creche and six balwadis in the surrounding Madia villages.

Wherever the Anganwadi scheme is running properly the Madia parents are sending children. But the impression gathered is that it is merely for the nutrition which is supplied.

The Anganwadi worker gets an Honorarium and as such there is no guarantee of job to her. In fact she is not an 'employee' of the Government at all. One senior C.D.P.O. described the position as a social-worker hired by government on an honorarium. With hardly Rs. 250 to Rs. 300 as honorarium they don't get competent girls. In this area tribal girls are selected as they know the dialect and can easily establish rapport with tribal mothers and children.

The posts of Supervisor, Medical Officer, Nurses lie vacant for months or years together.

The food material purchased from market is not up to mark. It was reported that the *Chana* (Gram) purchased from shops is half eaten by moths, or the consignment — which is less in weight — is sent to the concerned office — then it reaches the Anganwadi and is again returned to the shop-keeper who returns the amount to the functionary. On the stock-book the entries are neatly and properly maintained. At one place, on sudden inspection, it was found out by an officer of other Department that the names of pregnant women to whom Sukhda was distributed were almost similar for 3 consecutive years. This was strange and the Anganwadi worker conceded that they were bogus and the real stuff was distributed to influential persons. All these malpractices are going on and there is either no supervision or purposeful connivance. Though the C.D.P.O. has a Jeep and a driver, it is always out of headquarters for going to other towns and not so much in the area of his project. It is surprising to note that for 2-3 years C.D.P.O.s have not visited some centres. Posts of Medical Officer (who should be M.B.B.S.) are vacant and the scheme depends upon the bounty of the Doctor of the P.H.C. The A.N.M. (Auxiliary Nurse-cum-Midwife) is probably the only functionary who manages the health aspects.

Thus, though the response of the Madias is good the scheme is unable to work properly and meet the needs of the community. The Madia women are development-oriented and if the programme is properly implemented it can get very good response and contribute in improving the health standards of children in the area.

Successfully Implemented Schemes with Good Response and Output

Out of the various individual beneficiary schemes implemented, the following were properly implemented and had good response and results were obviously good.

Bhamragad I.T.D.P. (Primitive Tribes) Area

1. *Sewing Machines*

This was a scheme in which the beneficiary actually received the benefit and the two beneficiaries studied were using it for earning wages and supporting their families. The machines were of good make and giving good service. The local people also got the benefit of tailoring service.

2. *Supply of Utensils, Woollen Blankets etc.*

This scheme was properly implemented and proved very useful to satisfy their family needs.

3. *Supply of Goats, Poultry, Chicks etc.*

This scheme was not widely implemented but wherever it was, the results were good and rewarding to the beneficiary.

4. *Training in Animal Husbandry etc.*

The scheme implemented through the concerned Department's unit at Bhamragad was very nicely implemented. The unit with its exhibits, animal farms etc. at Bhamragad is nicely maintained. The Madia youths were trained in animal husbandry and dairy work for a month with Rs. 300 stipend per trainee. Each trained trainee received a cow, a calf and a goat in some cases. In some villages they also supplied a breeding-bull for a group of trainees from one village. Fodder and mineral mixture was also supplied for some months.

As a follow-up of the scheme, milk-cans and cycles were given to those boys, so that they can sale milk in the nearby places like Bhamragad.

This scheme was in fact against the tradition of Madias. They don't milk cows/buffaloes etc. as it is tabooed by their tradition. They also don't consume milk. While asked, some beneficiaries under this scheme told that they now milk the cows, and sell and at times (though rarely) drink milk. The acceptance of this scheme is a departure from the position about 12-15 years ago (sometime around 1975-76) when the Madias in this area were given Haryana breed cows and provision for grass-plots was also made by Forest Department. But as the Madias did not milk the cows they either dried-up or died. The only shortcoming in the present scheme is absence of the follow-up by giving medical help to cows and supply of fodder on a continuing basis where it is not available.

But on the whole the scheme is well coordinated, honestly implemented and good. As the cow is insured, in the cases of its death the share of the tribal beneficiary is borne by the Insurance Agency.

5. *Scheme for the Supply of 'Prakashtha-Upakarans' to Madia Tribals*

Implemented by the Forest Department, each beneficiary under the scheme was given four items viz. *Kudal* (Pick-axe), *Favada* (Spade), *Ghamela* (Iron-pan) and *Sabbal* (Crow-bar). The title of the scheme is wrong. '*Prakashtha*' should mean, 'concerned with wood-work or carpentry'. The Divisional Forest Officer agreed that he also thought like that but the Secretariat people clarified the point by detailing the above implements. The scheme was properly implemented and the beneficiaries could either work on their own farms or could get the support of these implements for doing labour-work in forest.

6. *Scheme for Organising Madia's Marriages*

This scheme meant payment of marriage expenses to youths for their marriages. This was properly implemented.

7. *Trip of Madias to Various Places*

Trips of Madia boys and girls were organised to Nagpur, Chandrapur, Warora etc. In previous years they were even taken to Bombay. The scheme had good impact on the troupe. They became aware, alert, and it helped in accelerating awareness and acculturation of the group.

8. *Ploughing of Madias' Land by Tractor*

This was really a well-conceived scheme but could not be properly implemented. Madia-Gonds and particularly the Bada or Hill Madias who were traditionally, shifting cultivators, were sowing by 'broadcast' method because ploughing on the 'bosom of mother earth' was tabooed in their tribe. On this background it was interesting to know that even in villages where the shifting cultivators were settled, they welcomed this scheme. As discussed earlier, it was the agency/department operating this scheme which fell short in fulfilling their expectations. The tractor operator told that there should be large units of land. The Madia tribals who are still living a real community life were even ready to remove fences of farms and allow ploughing by tractor for the whole village lands. They also demanded it every year as doing it only for one year was not useful and may create problems for them. At one place the tractor driver could not plough properly as the land was too hard. Later they ploughed it by conventional method of ploughing. Similarly, when land is ploughed by tractor, more water is essential for land. On the whole the scheme is good and is well-accepted by tribals. Follow-up is essential.

9. *Improvement of Madia-Farmers' Lands/Construction of Bodis*

This scheme was implemented on a very small scale — hardly in a couple of villages. The scheme essentially was levelling and bunding of land. Local farmers/villagers were asked to do earth-work and levelling work and were paid for their labour. This scheme can be further expanded, but, payment of wages must be proper and as per the figures shown in the budget of the scheme.

Construction of *Bodis* (rain water reservoirs by digging and bunding) was also implemented in a few villages. This also should get priority. The tribals welcome it and it can raise agriculture out-put.

Implementation of Schemes — A Review Needed

Schemes should be made local-based and independent of outsiders. Let us consider a few schemes in the light of the earlier findings.

Roofing Tiles

These need not be Manglore tiles. They should be of the local-made (*Gav rani*) tiles and the tribal village near sources of water should be entrusted with its manufacture. The Gaita/Patel should be entrusted with it. Some training could be given to local villagers and tiles produced near village in small kilns. These villages will be centres for supplying these tiles to the villages in vicinity. They can carry these tiles in their own bullock-carts. These tiles then will be easily replaced when damaged and the villagers will be independent of officers, M.S.T.D.C. and the corruption due to contractors could be eliminated (Tiles were quoted at Rs. 140 to 170 per 100 while they could be easily obtained @Rs. 110 per 100. This was reported to me by a high state government officer).

Bullock-carts

Wood is available in the forest. The Forest Department is having logging centres and log-depots in all areas. The Punjabrao Krishi Vidyapeeth had introduced a scheme of giving training to tribals in carpentry. Through some such scheme village artisans should be asked to prepare bullock-carts for the group of villagers. The wood will be available in the area. As electrification is in progress the Forest Department should be asked to instal a few saw-mills in the area. Cut-size pieces will be given to rural artisans who will prepare the carts and artisan will be paid suitable wages. The iron tyres for carts can also be prepared locally by providing iron belts to tribal black-smiths. Thus complete bullock carts could be given to villagers in surrounding area. The Animal Husbandry unit at Bhamragad can supply pairs of bullocks. The bullock-pairs and carts should be given simultaneously. All Government and other agencies should be asked to give labour work to the Madias, whenever their work in the area is to be done. Apart from providing local employment and eliminating all intermediaries/contractors (and thereby scope for corruption), we can create local employment and give fillip to the traditional capacities of tribals who are idle.

Animal Husbandry

While giving cows, bullocks etc. those breeds which can withstand local climatic and environmental conditions need only be given. It is useless to transplant a Haryana cow who is accustomed to a particular type of diet and care to these primitive tribals. The result has been that it goes on weakening day by day and dies. Even the milk-giving capacity goes down within 2-3 months.

Grass-lands should be developed in the forest adjoining each village which will supply fodder to cattle. These could be developed by Forest Department.

Mechanical Inputs

When cycles, sewing machines and oil/electric pumps are given it will be desirable to organise a three-day training programme in minor repairs followed with giving a kit of spanners, accessories etc. While giving oil/electric engines the pipe requirement should be ascertained and pipe given along wit the pump.

A persistent complaint has been of diesel, problem of repairs to pumps and even to government vehicles. Even the government officers are held up and when they go to Allapalli for Petrol (about 125 Km both ways) that much of petrol is wasted. It is advisable to start a workship with Petrol/Diesel Pump at Bhamragad which will supply petrol/diesel and also render repairs/servicing to government vehicles as well as to oil/electric pumps etc. This workshop-cum-servicing Centre should be started by the State Government. It can also do private business by supply of services to private vehicles like those of B.I.L.T.

Madia-women and Development Schemes

As discussed earlier, the Madia women have huge potentials for development. It seems that neither the T.S.P. schemes nor those specially evolved under nucleus budget have an accent on womens' development. Except the I.C.D.S. there is no consideration of women as a group in the process. It will be worthwhile to plan schemes covering health, hygiene, prevention of diseases, child care, nutrition etc. and operate them for women.

Similarly bamboo-craft, dancing and singing, preparation of pickles, jams and jellies from the forest fruits, preservation of fruits etc. can be used for preparation of schemes for women from all areas of Madia habitat. It women will be involved their families and villages can be easily involved in development.

6

ATTITUDES AND OPINIONS

Views of Leaders and Officers

Tribal leaders and officers expressed the following views on the various schemes and their implementation.

The Leaders

The traditional tribal leadership in the area is not much favourable to development. The feudal mentality still persists which is averse to development, the ostensible and plausible reason given being that development will expose the primitive tribals more to outside world thus giving scope to more exploitation — social and economic — and of women and men. They are opposed to building bridges on big rivers like the Bandiya and to all-season roads within the area.

Industrialisation in and around the area is also opposed. They now support education, prohibition, health services and agricultural inputs and occupations related to farming. They also support minor irrigation but oppose big dams.

The younger lot is of a different type. They invite development and criticise old leaders. Exploitation of tribals is opposed by them, at times, in an organised manner but this is more so in the Etapalli I.T.D.P area.

The Officers

Those at the State level (barring a few exceptions) harbour a romanticism feeling that they should provide all sophisticated and modern facilities to these tribals (one officer said "we are going to provide their children the best possible convent-type education like our children in the cities"). One state level officer asked as to why should they go and live in secluded remote villages on hills and forests? Why should they not be brought to neighbouring areas rather than reaching development to such remote places?

Some officers working in the field have good and real assessment of their life and problems but among the field officers some had not even visited some parts/villages irrespective of the fact that it was the area of their work. Some felt that these poor tribals should be given economic and medical help with priority but some felt that they will never change and develop whatever may be the schemes.

It was also opined by some officers that giving aid free is of no use. They must be asked to contribute either in kind or cash so that they will know its value. One important implementing officer said that he had given them benefits and God only knows whether the benefits are with them or given away by them to others. All the field officers were critical and felt that their counterparts at the state level could not understand and appreciate their problems. On the contrary those at the state level felt that the officers in field did not give the correct and realistic picture of the situation to them.

Development oriented and optimistic outlook is found in very few officers in the field but many of them do work and implement schemes in which they themselves do not believe. It is only those few who have faith in a new dawn and the potentials of the tribals who are bringing out a dint of change.

Madias' Attitudes Towards Benefits and Attitudinal Changes

Out of the beneficiaries studied, 74 per cent had applied in some form or the other meaning thereby that they were interested in getting the benefit. While some were told about the benefit by the Organiser others came to know from their friends or local villagers. Again 74 per cent expressed a desire to get the continuation of the same benefit or its follow-up benefit. Thirty-five per cent of the beneficiaries felt benefited on getting the benefit while 56.52 per cent felt that the benefit had some favourable impact on their lives. The remaining beneficiaries who did not feel benefited were not dis-satisfied with the benefit as such, but because some relevant factor which could have helped them in taking advantage of the benefit was absent. A few typical cases can illustrate the point.

Madia-Gonds are traditionally against ploughing of land and as such used to sow seeds by broadcast method. When the scheme of ploughing their lands by tractors was implemented even all the Bada

(Hill) Media villagers accepted it. This indicates 100 per cent change of outlook in the group of beneficiaries to whom the scheme was applied. However their complaint was that due to hardness of land it was not properly ploughed and that there were no rains and hence they could not get the benefit. They even suggested levelling and bunding of land by bulldozers.

Another case was about the scheme of training in Animal Husbandry on stipend, followed with grant of a cow, calf, a milk-can and cycle. As per traditional Madia-culture milking cows or buffaloes is taboo and they don't drink and sell milk. However they welcomed training, accepted cows, took out milk and sold it @Rs. 4 per litre. Some youths told that they even drink it. The response was 100 per cent so far as training and milking cows was concerned, though so far as drinking of milk was concerned, it was 50 per cent that too in the younger generation. Their complaints were that the cows did not get grass and fodder and have gone weak, yield of milk dwindled, the milk did not have sufficient market etc. But they accepted the scheme.

The above two examples are indicative of the attitudinal changes perceptable in the Madias.

The scheme of trip to Nagpur was also appreciated and well received by all. This shows that they want to see outside world and have communication.

Even the oil engines — which is a technological in-put in a primitive culture was accepted by all beneficiaries (Response 100%). They even applied and some were awaiting to get one. Those who got diesel, and technical help when needed were growing fruit and vegetable garden, groundnut, tobacco etc. the problem was of getting pipe, diesel and of repairs. This also shows a basic attitudinal change and readyness to accept.

The schemes regarding sewing machines, and cycle-hire shops, though implemented on modest scale meaning thereby that only a few beneficiaries were covered, one has to conclude that they were 100 per cent successful. The sewing machines are being properly used and they are supporting their families by earning additional income. Same is true of cycle-hire shops. Both the schemes are also useful to others who take benefit of the services from these machines/cycles. The only care which could be taken in such schemes is that the necessary tool-box should be provided and same training in minor repairs of these machines be imparted.

The three benefits which not only all the beneficiaries who were interviewed liked but the whole village craved for, were Bullock-pairs, Bullock-carts and tiles for roofing. Here they complained of irregularities, harassment, quality of carts and bullocks, absence of timely help of veterinary doctor and quality of tiles. It is interesting to note that in a few Madia villages almost all beneficiaries got themselves operated for family planning to get tiles. This definitely indicates that they very much wanted roofing tiles.

More Production — The Only Solution

The above discussion clearly points out to the fact that better in-puts in agricultural production and improving the labour capacities of the Madia-farmers is the only solution to their problems. The attitudinal changes perceptible in their behaviour and views should be properly utilised by the development administration. Ploughing of lands, timely distribution of seeds and manures, bodis, oil-pumps or other irrigation facilities, agricultural implements, bullocks and carts — all this given as a package-deal will be accepted by the people and utilised for their own development. This is the only viable solution.

Developing a will 'To Develop'

The basic problem is of complacency. An otherwise laudable characteristic but not in the area of tribal development is the problem of fewer wants of the tribals. They are apathetic and idle because they have very few wants. They are not attracted to earning more because the ideas of surplus production, more income, savings and investment are not present in their mind. If their primary wants of food, shelter and clothing are satisfied they are happy. The idleness and consequent complacency born out of the meagreness of wants is an obstruction to development. The administrators and social workers must try to create a desire in them for a fuller and better life with more wants. This will create an urge to develop, work more and take advantage of the benefit schemes. This can be done by exposing them to the outside world, improving communications, organising result demonstrations, exhibitions, fairs in the interior parts and giving them quick, clean and unhampered services. The examples are there which indicate that this is possible. They demand tiles for roofing, agricultural in-puts and ploughing, medical services, cows and bullocks etc. Such attitudinal changes should be studied and other schemes can be implemented on the same pattern.

The administration will also have to fulfil their demands and should not lag behind.

A Polyvalent, Forestry-based Integrated Development Model*

Model suggested by Shri V.K. Mohan, Divisional Forest Officer and implemented on trial basis in village Erandgaon of District Nasik is worth considering. This model shows as to how the well established infrastructure of the Forest Department can be used for development purpose.

The different schemes implemented by the Government, the development and utilisation of non-conventional energy resources, forest nursery and fuel wood, bio-gas plants, fodder resources, nurseries for forest and domestic plantation and for bio-mass production etc. are all developed on an area of about 40 hectares (with irrigation) covering a group of villages. The labour inputs will be from the tribals. Resource-inputs from the forest and relevant government Departments and the out-put to be utilised for the tribal population. Such polyvalent units may be established in each of the Revenue Circle in the Bhamragad I.T.D. area.

---

* Please see Appendix V for the details of the Scheme.

RESTRUCTURING THE MODEL

In the light of the foregoing analysis, it is evident that the Tribal Sub-Plan schemes have been implemented in the area under study (i.e. the primitive tribal areas in the Gadchiroli district i.e. the I.T.D.P. (Primitive Tribes) specially at Bhamragad), and the new structures have been experimented with sincerity.

The Tribal Sub-Plan schemes are implemented but the new structures created are not yet firmly rooted. The Adiwasi Cooperative Societies (ACSs) have became almost defunct. The Ashram- school Complex and the 'Growth Centres' have not taken the forms which were envisaged in the earlier blue-print. The Project Office and the T.D.O. office are functioning, the Gram Panchayats are dissolved and fresh elections are not held and as such the new structures are not firmly rooted. The Madia-Gond Tribals in the area have been economically benefited as a result of the schemes under the T.S.P. though not with maladies.

Though the beneficiaries have been benefited by almost all the schemes (barring a few exceptions like the ploughing of land or gobar-gas plants) and if the shortcomings or lacunae are removed they can get still better benefits.

It can be said that the tribals have responded favourably to the schemes under T.S.P. in general as almost all the beneficiaries have welcomed the scheme, have complained for not getting benefits and have even gone to the extent of giving Rs. 2 per head to the organiser. The analysis of their attitudes proves this point.

Consequently, the social life of the tribals has also changed towards better living as a result of the schemes implemented under the T.S.P. but this has not been uniform in all areas.

Traditionally, the Madia are accustomed to a social life based on community living and brotherhood. Their culture is rich. The schemes implemented only touch the outer and physical aspects of social life. On the contrary the distribution of benefits to some of them is likely to create 'haves' and 'have-nots' and the organic unity of Madia life is likely to be disturbed. It is better if, as suggested earlier, schemes are given to the village community as such and when individual beneficiaries are to be covered all households from that village ought to be covered and benefit given. If harassment, exploitation and the occasional corruption in implementation is stopped, the probabilities of spoiling their social life will decrease. Even this will be an achievement.

The physical and environmental aspects of their life have improved e.g. better housing, drinking water, health services, Anganwadis/schools, better roads etc. as a result of the schemes, and to that extent the social life, as expressed in 'better living'. But much remains to be done in bettering their living conditions.

By way of conclusion it can be said that the basic concepts and the administrative structure of Tribal Sub-Plan conceived initially was extremely good. However it could not be translated in its true spirits to the tribal soil. Subsequent changes at the operational level created two diametrically opposite defects viz. overlapping of machinery of various departments for the same beneficiaries and benefits on one side and lack of coordination between two or more departments and their functionaries on the other side. A true integration has not yet been effected in spite of the creation of the office of the Commissioner for Tribal Development. Thus, the administrative bottle-necks, combined with the paucity of dedicated administrations with reliable integrity carried the whole endeavour into doldrums. The primitive tribals who were initially averse to development were ultimately awakened and enthused to accept and utilise the benefits of development but then the administrative machinery and infrastructure fell miserably short in fulfilling the rising expectations. Lack of development-oriented leadership in the primitive tribe and their ignorance, corruption, and the tendency to 'achieve' pre-determined and ordained targets gave rise to bogus implementation at many places.

Lack of dedicated and rather committed personnel in the development administration coupled with total absence of an elite among the tribals who could represent their interests, complaints etc. came in the way of a true and productive implementation even of the well-planned schemes.

Many schemes reached the tribal areas but could not spread to the remotest corners. Follow-up was also not adequate for all the schemes. The local tribal youths, local and traditional leaders could sense and smell smack but did not dare to come forward to lodge complaints. Even among the beneficiaries, the more 'powerful' or 'influential' could get better benefits.

With more schemes with a local need and production base, more positive involvement of local tribals, the proper utilisation of their age-old community spirit and a team of young, dedicated and non-corrupt promoters/administrators, the instrument of Tribal Sub-Plan could be used in a better manner to bring the dreams of Pt. Jawaharlal Nehru and Dr. Verrier Elwin into reality.

New Trend

A new trend is seen in the personnel policy sine 1989-90 when a batch of Project Officers was appointed in the I.T.D.Ps. The recruitment policy insisted on formal educational qualifications in Social Work and some previous experience of working in tribal areas. Thus, the Project Officers for the I.T.D.P., Etapalli, Bhamragad etc. are holders of Masters Degrees in Social Work, with experience of working in Tribal areas. When the author conducted a continuing Education Course in Legal Awareness for Madia-Gond youths he saw the difference in the style of working of these officers and their approach to tribals. Such changes are welcome for development.

Suggestions for Policy Formulation

The Administrative Organisation

The Integrated Tribal Development Programme was planned basically on the ideology of 'integrated' treatment whether of the area, the population or the administration. The structures envisaged in the initial approach never came into reality.

The Growth Centre idea remained on paper and the Ashram School Complex was also not created. It was just an Ashram School meaning a school with a hostel.

The Adivasi Co-operative Societies which were created and linked with M.S.T.D. Corporation with the hopes to provide an infrastructure for economic growth and as centres for the sale purchase of products, and for providing credit facilities to tribals ran into trouble, lost their financial viability and were unable to make payments to tribals. Monopolistic purchase of paddy entrusted to these societies resulted into hardships to tribals as they could not make payments to tribals nor could the tribals sell paddy to merchants. The societies went into liquidation and even the price of paddy purchased earlier is yet to be paid to tribals. The ACSs are now defunct. The M.S. Tribal Development Corporation is not performing some functions properly.

The administrative organisation under a Tribal Commissioner should have provided a unified approach, but even this could not be achieved. Multiplicity of agencies/Departments function in the same area for the same people and at times giving similar benefits. In case of bullock-carts, the M.S.T.D. Corporation, the Forest Department are both operating the scheme, the Project Officer keeping only the records. The oil/electric pump scheme is operated by the Tribal Development Officer, and pumps are provided by the M.S.T.D.C. The bank officials also come into picture where a part of the finance is to be met through bank loans. The Project Officer has no special powers. His work is mostly keeping records. He is unable to bring out cooperation between various departments/agencies working in the same field. Except for a few schemes from Nucleus Budget funds and S.C.A. funds he just consolidates the figures spent through various departments. The Forest Department, M.S. Electricity Board, even the Panchayat Samiti and the I.C.D.S. personnel — all work independently of each other. The common terminology used by these officers is 'your' and 'my' department and not 'our' department.

The Project Office staff is inadequate. Posts are vacant for years together. The post of the Project Officer at I.T.D.P., Etapalli, is lying vacant since 31-7-1984 and only 'In-charge' persons are working. The Bhamragad I.T.D.P. was previously under an Assistant Project Officer, but during 1985-86 the post was upgraded to that of Project Officer. The P.O. Bhamragad has one Head Clerk/Accountant, one typist, one Statistical Assistant, a peon and a driver. The staff appeared to be sluggish and the Statistical Assistant is a drunkard who is always down with wine. He rarely attends office and is lying senseless in his quarters. The P.O. complained that he is of no use to him but on humanitarian grounds no action is taken against him.

The Project-cum-Block Development Officer of Etapalli Panchayat Samiti has to look after both the T.D. Blocks — Etapalli and Bhamragad — and as such both the Project areas are covered. He was complaining of inadequate staff. The Bhamragad T.D. Block which was created long back and received special Central Government grants remained on paper and separate or even adequate Block staff was never appointed. The Project-cum-Block Development Officer is having one jeep which is old and mostly out of use and he said he cannot visit far-off areas in secluded places like those on the Laheri hills and M.P. Border. There seems to be no coordination between the work done by the P.C.B.D.O. and the Project Officer. The C.D.P.O. of the I.C.D.S. also functions in his own sphere without much coordination with sister departments in spite of the fact that the charge of the P.C.B.D.O. is with the C.D.P.O. of I.C.D.S. when there is no incumbent on that post. The Tribal Development Officer, Aheri has got his own establishment — a pretty big one, and operates his schemes independently. All these officers have jeeps and other staff but is not useful for each other. For example when the C.D.P.O. or T.D.O.s' Jeep is available and moves in the area the P.C.B.D.O. cannot go for visits as there is no coordination between these offices. The Forest Department is having an excellent infrastructure in the remotest corners of the area. They have their staff quarters, offices and all the functionaries are found at their proper places. They have good rapport with the tribal people and with all said and done about that department, one has to admit that they have the requisite man power competent and suitable for working in the tribals.

The Deputy Commissioner (Tribal) who is also the Collector of the District is a functionary so overburdened with work – particularly law and order problems, that he simply *cannot* pay sufficient attention and look into the I.T.D.P. work and effect coordination.

The staff in these development departments is mostly a grumbling lot cursing their own fate and the Government for sending to remote tribal areas. Many are sent on punishment. As a result, 90 per cent employees are seen to do either or many of the following things:

(i) Don't join the post for months together, defying the transfer order.

(ii) Don't stay at headquarters and always go to their towns or other places — many times showing that they are on tour in some remote secluded area (they are sure that no superior can pay a surprise visit nor can any one verify by going to the spot).

(iii) Stay at the headquarters, indulge in drinking, exploiting tribals, taking undue advantages (including that from women) do farming on others' or encroached land, mis-use Departments' resources like personal property, take bribes and illegal Commissions from the contractors/traders etc., who have had transactions with the Department, and some even establish their huge fortunes starting their own business etc. This type is then ready to stickup to the area and does not grumble.

(iv) Basically good but a lot disturbed and frustrated as wife and children are at townships and cities for children's education and at a ripe age they have to lead a lonely life in tribal areas.

It is only that 10 per cent marginal lot which runs the departments' activity and does something good for the poor tribals. They are noble exceptions but often become eye-sores for their impious colleagues.

The Commissioners and Collectors often say that they don't get the correct picture and when they asked me I told them that they visit the area with their fleet of jeeps, full of officers, are always in great hurry, talk with the tribals in the presence of an army officer in a purely formal and sophisticated urban manner. How can the poor tribals dare to spell out their real woes? And what about the victimisation with vengeance to which they will be exposed after the big boss returns to his headquarters in cities?

The Recruitment Policy

When Community Development Programme was started the Government of India had emphasised the need of 'developmental' approach as against the 'revenue' approach. As such the posting of revenue officers in development departments and that too in such sensitive areas is against the development philosophy. Those who may be successful in achieving family planning operations targets and augmenting deposits for small savings may not necessarily be successful in ushering in development. Similarly some sense of dedication and humanitarian outlook is a pre-requisite for working in this field.

There is a need to change our total approach to recruitment for development. As Dr. Paul Appleby said long-back, recruitment ought to be "aggressive and imaginative". Rules of selection may have to be relaxed if work is to be done and 'goods delivered'. It is not difficult to get young (or middle aged) persons from outside the Government or even from within the Government (may be they are in any other Department) who will volunteer to go to these areas and enjoy the thrill of serving the downtrodden humanity. It should be possible to advertise in newspapers, on TV and radio (not in the usual legalistic and prosaic manner of other Government advertisements but like a private company, in an attractive manner) and to invite such persons to accept the challenge of working in this area on a contract basis say of 2 to 5 years. If necessary, these selected persons should be given some orientation training in Anthropology and Development at some National Institutes like those at Hyderabad, New Delhi or Mussoorie, and then post them on contract.

As a matter of policy — whether for newly selected or the departmental ones — those who are unmarried or newly married or with children whose schooling has not started should be sent to the area. Good work in the area, the assessment of which will depend upon the change in the tribal life — should be rewarded. One must remember that each Department, scheme, clientele will need different type of workers, and hence recruitment to be productive, must consider the above points. The puritanic and orthodox attitude of the Secretariat will not help. Similarly the myth that persons from the tribal communities will serve the tribals better is also exploded and they have proved as good and as bad as any one else. The attitude depends upon individual 'persons' and not on anything else. So, all the traditional legal-institutional 'myths' nursed and pampered in our Departments should give way to a strict 'behavioural' and 'communications' approach.

A Really Integrated Set-up —An Organisational Set-up Suggested

An administrative organisation may be adopted, as suggested in the flow-chart.

In this set-up the Additional Chief Secretary who will also be the Secretary T.D.D. and Tribal Commissioner, should have supreme power to sanction any scheme/programmes irrespective of the Department concerned. For example, within the limits of the total Budget sanction, if he approved of a scheme concerning Forest or P.W.D. or Education, etc., there shall be no need of concurrence from that Department and only sending a copy for information to that office and to their Chief in the area will be sufficient. Thus, the work will proceed without further delay. The Project Development Officer will then instruct the concerned officer working under him

FLOW-CHART

ORGANISATIONAL SET-UP — SUGGESTED

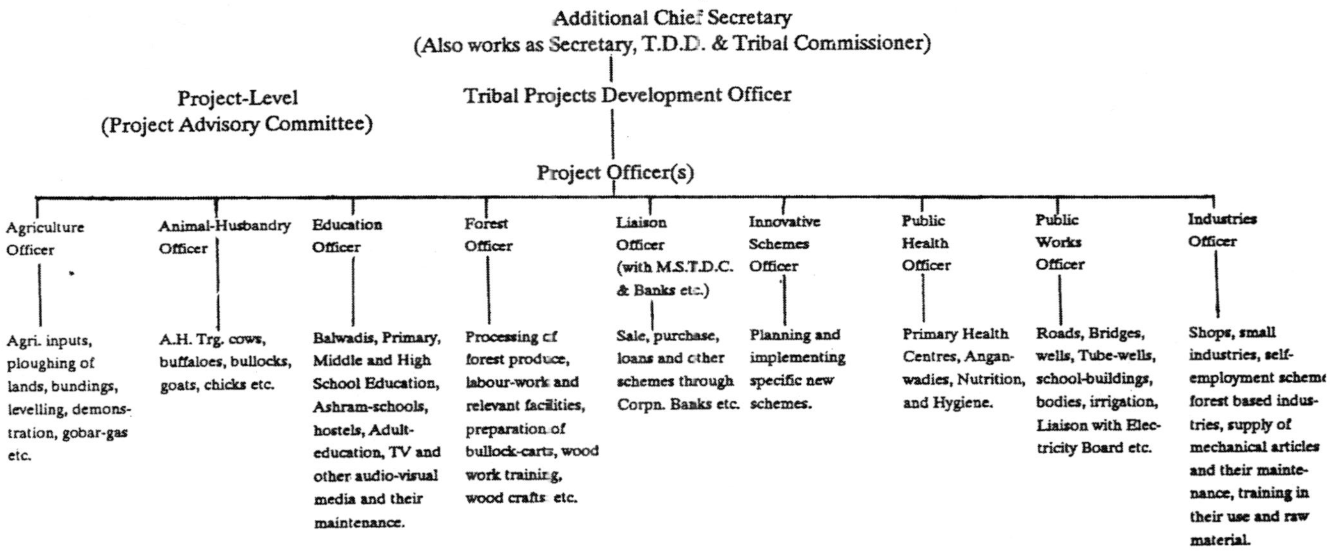

Note: For functions of the higher officers please see pages 154-155.

and it will be the duty of the concerned Departments' Officer working in that area to cooperate and implement the scheme. He need not wait for clearance from his bosses.

The Project Development Officer will plan, suggest and supervise the whole work and take advice of the Project Advisory Committee and act as liaison between the Project Officer and the Commissioner. The Project Officer will be the Chief implementing authority with a team of nine officers among whom the work will be distributed.

All the above officers and even their supporting staff should be drawn from the best lot after scrutiny of their reports and these posts should be offered as promotional posts. After showing good-results in the areas, further promotion could be promised. Those who have their families with children studying in schools and colleges should be given rent-free accommodation in those towns and special facilities for visiting them once a month. The morale of staff must be kept up.

The functions of the higher officers shown in the flow chart and the constitution of the project level committee will be as follows:

(1) The Additional Chief Secretary to the Government will also works as Secretary Tribal Development Department and Tribal Commissioner, will do the work of coordination of the different development departments at the State level and his approval for any scheme shall be deemed to be the approval from the concerned department. He will guide and supervise the whole set-up.

(2) The Project Advisory Committee which will be at the project level shall consist of Tribal M.L. As and leaders of different parties from that area, Anthropologists, social workers, some renowned physicians/surgeons, Collector of the district, C.E.O. of Zilla Parishad, President of Z.P. and Chairman of Social Welfare Committee, Chairman of Panchayat Samiti and some Representatives of the prominent educational institution from the area.

(3) Tribal Projects Development Officer shall be at the project level and will be of the rank of Deputy Commissioner Tribal i.e. Collector. He will be Ex-officio Member-Secretary of the Project Advisory Committee. He will be responsible for overall coordination of different development departments at the project level and shall be responsible for planning and implementation of the schemes. He should be a person with an aptitude and background of working in tribal area and with

a successful record of work which should be ascertained before posting. In all cases some orientation training in Anthropology and Tribal Development ought to be given. His headquarters must be in the project area.

(4) Project Officer — this officer will be directly Incharge of the implementation of schemes in the project area. Preferably he should be a man either from the Forest Department or with background of working in tribal populations in some voluntary organisation and must be given some training in Anthropology and Tribal Development and in Extension methods. He will supervise and coordinate the work of nine 'subject-matter specialist' officers and will also be the Chief disbursing officer for them. The proposed petrol/diesel pump-cum-servicing work-shop will be under his control. On his recommendations the Tribal Projects Development Officer will take action whose decision shall be final except review by the Secretary and Tribal Commissioner in extra-ordinary circumstances.

8

TRIBAL CULTURE AND DEVELOPMENT

Tribal culture has been a matter of interest and attraction for the outside cultures but so far the so-called 'stronger cultures' have not properly and fully understood its content and nature. Man is considered a part and parcel of the environment and the tribal communities are — to a large extent — really a part of nature. Early individualism was overtaken by socialism and man as a part of society acquired different status, rights and duties. The tribal man/woman is not only intrinsic part of the tribal community but also of the Nature including trees, animals, birds even rocks, mountains, rivers etc. There is a perfect symbiotic relationship preserved historically which is both — interdependent and reciprocal. This harmony of life and recognition of equality of the *raison de etre* of existence of all is reflected in their animism, festivals, folk-lore and in the totality of culture. The aspects of preservation of the community and of the natural environment, its optimum use, change and development are all discernible to a student of tribal culture.

Considering the basic needs of food, shelter and clothing one finds that they are minimum and dependent on local environment. While the tribals from the Central and Southern parts of India with hot climates put-on just a lion cloth, those in the Himalayan region put-on profuse and coloured dresses of woollen or other organic fibres. The simple thatched hut with mud-covered bamboo walls is the minimum which the tribal has been successfully using for years. Though, originally they are non-vegetarians, they have never killed animals except for satisfying hunger. Similarly, though they are fully dependent on forest for housing, fuel, medicinal needs and other wants, wanton felling of trees (for commercial purposes) has never been undertaken, and, in fact, before the advent of the British regime they were the original conservators of forest. Their economy has been a subsistence economy without commercial out-look. To use Aristotelian concept of property, one may describe, their production and consumption pattern as 'natural' being only for local use and not for exchange. *Chrematistics*, which Aristotle brands as worst than brigandage, was not practised by most of the tribals.

One important factor in connection with the question of basic needs of man should be interesting. In all tribal communities 'sex' has been recognised as one of the basic needs and this awareness is present not only at an individual level but in the whole community, and, special institutions, procedures and solutions were evolved to harness it. The youth dormitories, rituals on attainment of puberty, different methods of selecting life-partners, freedom given to girls, the ritual of marriage, polygynny (polyandry is now obsolete), facilities and procedures for divorce and remarriage, certain taboos and occasions to use abusive language in a 'healthy' manner etc., are all instances which show that rather than suppressing 'sex' they have institutionalised it with proper social control. Absence of child marriage and the institution of bride-price are indicators of realism as well as the economic significance of women.

Tribal women are economic assets to the family and society. They work hard and contribute to production — at home, in farms and also do hard manual labour for earning bread. They are more active, enthusiastic, alert and development-oriented as compared to men who are relatively lazy and sluggish. In most tribal communities silver ornaments (gold is rare) are profusely used by women in addition to beads, flowers etc. The scanty clothing used by many tribal women is often interpreted as a sign of their poverty. This is not always so. Even the wife of a Mukhiya/Patel who has many acres of land, and has profuse silver ornaments on her body keeps her breasts uncovered, not because she has no money to purchase a blouse or a piece of cloth but because it is tradition, a way of life. Our development schemes have not tapped and provided for the potentials of tribal women. She is going as labour on public works and forests and stakes her modesty. Handicrafts, painting, cottage industries based on local products, music and dance and social welfare activities for the community are some areas in which the tribal women can be profitably and hopefully involved in future.

Community spirit in socio-cultural occasions is also reflected in their economic life. More primitive the tribe, more socialistic is its economic life. They live in a spirit of sharing and not of grabbing or exploiting each other. Honesty, non-possession and mutual help are the typical characteristics of tribal socio-economic life. Barter was an institution born out of mutual trust and help. When any benefit was obtained they all shared it equitably. The Panchayat (traditional, not statutory) looked after the differences and its decisions were unanimously accepted. The traditional Panchayats could administer justice. They were known for their impartial decision and the whole community had full faith in them. Even the severe punishments administered by them were accepted by all. It is interesting to observe that the statutory Panchayats created after democratic decentralisation could not create the same image. Groupism, party-spirit, bickerings and a sense of unjust actions characterised these Panchayats. In spite of the statutory sanctions, the 'real' wills of the community members could not came-up and prevail to create a 'general will' in the interest of the whole community. On the contrary the traditional Panchayats — wherever functionary – still display the magnanimity of the community spirit and action. This phenomenon needs further study.

However, there were areas in which the tribals needed assistance and services. For example, health services, education to children, provision of consumption articles at reasonable rates (e.g., salt, match-boxes, kerosene, edible oils etc.) in their villages, agricultural inputs, and all weather communication facilities with outside world may be mentioned as some of the areas. The schemes for development have done much, though, much more needs to be done. In the foregoing pages attempt has been made to take stock of some of the schemes. One important factor assumes importance in this context. What has been the impact of the development schemes on the fibre of tribal culture which was simple, straight and clean as briefly described above. A few observations made by the author are given below.

The schemes could not be made applicable to all households/ individuals though, all may be needy. The administrators selected a few from each village. This created 'haves' and the 'have-nots'. In a society where even a small benefit used to be shared on a community basis, now we have applied schemes under which a few get the benefits, giving rise to unequal treatment, heart-burning and frictions. As this is many times done on an arbitrary basis the dis-satisfaction increases. Are we replacing their traditional 'primitive socialism' by our modern brand of distributive socialism?

Creation of a desire for a better and fuller life with more wants is essential if the tribals are to be attracted to the schemes for economic betterment. However this has also resulted in a rat-race for getting benefits and greed as against minimum wants, and dishonesty (sown simultaneously with schemes by the agents for development) as against traditional honesty is setting in the tribal life.

Schemes are not envisaged keeping in view the corporate structure of the tribal community which accounts for the failure or partial success of the scheme. To site a few examples, community gobar-gas plants, tractor ploughing of the farms of all villagers on a community basis, with supervision of the elders' council/traditional panchayats etc. could have been successful. A few officers have experimented with such schemes in Nagaland with great success. The traditional community centres and the community spirit should have been harnessed for this purpose. Result demonstrations at village/community level attract people's attention and develop a conviction on its efficacy.

Follow-up of many schemes has been either poor or totally absent. As a result, the tribal was not only up-rooted from his traditional method but was also kept away from the new thing/service creating misery. The monopoly purchase schemes for paddy, mahua flowers and other minor forest produce etc. are some of the instances. Either the payments were delayed for months together or not made at all and the private traders also refused to accept the produce. Distribution of exotic breeds of cattle, unsuitable to the environment and locally available fodder resulted in high death rate of the cattle. A modest scheme best suitable to the local environment and locally available material,with regular follow-up and support is more beneficial than technically best but unsuitable scheme. The Gobar-gas scheme, most suitable and useful to tribals failed due to faulty implementation and absence of follow-up.

It is essential to study and anticipate the teething trouble when we are implanting new ideas, introducing technology or making other in-puts in a culture-pattern which is far behind the modern culture-pattern, specially in the economic and technological aspects. The tribal culture still maintains a value-system which is rich in concepts and oriented to the spiritual and social norms. Even we the so-called progressives from modern culture-need to study and imbibe from them some good aspects, if we want to succeed in our ideal of creating a welfare state. On the contrary we are cutting them (the tribals) from their cultural moorings and tying them to things and forms which are neither reliable nor permanent. It is like banning consumption of *Toddy* or *Mahua* and giving permission (to outsiders) to open country liquor shops in/near the tribal areas. We are taking him for a ride on a road, which no one knows, and leave him stranded on it, grappling in the dark. He is at the mercy of the bureaucrat, trader-money lender, exploiters, politicians and terrorists.

Benthamite formula of the 'felicific calculus' needs to be adopted while formulating and implementing schemes in tribal areas. While commenting upon Bentham's 'greatest happiness of the greatest number' principle, Prof. Sabine said that it is the "greatest solvent of fictions, for it means that the real significance of law or an institution must be judged in terms of *what is does* (emphasis added), and so far possible *what it does* (emphasis added) to specific individuals". Thus, while planning and implementing a scheme the planners must consider the probable 'mischiefs' of its implementation and of not-implementing it in the context of the present situation of tribal culture, and, if the 'positive mischiefs' are probably more, it may be accepted. Every scheme must be properly, timely and fully implemented with steady follow-up till it becomes a part and parcel of the changed tribal practices. Touch-and-go treatment is likely to cause more damage to their socio-economic life than do any good. Feed-back of all schemes should be carefully considered and necessary changed accepted without being dogmatic on our pre-conceived notions.

Last, but not the least, is the knowledge of tribal dialect and codification in Devnagri/Roman scripts. This will bring out the rich treasure of tribal folk-lore and facilitate better communication between the agents of development and the tribal communities.

Cultural changes are setting-in very fast. Tribal culture has been an amalgam of social, economic and political components, and when the process of cultural change commences, mutation starts in all institutions, norms, mores and the totality of community life. Some new things are gained and some good old things are lost. While harmful superstitions give way, the useful herbal medicines are also lost. When forest based industries provide employment, the bio-mass of forest is destroyed. When traditional exploitation is checked new 'exploiters' take the place. When food habits change, there is lack of sufficient food and even of fuel to cook it. If the thatched huts are replaced by tiled ones, there is no supply of Mangalore tiles when required. When we increase his wants and introduce him to a money economy, all that simplicity born out of non-possession and the consequent honesty is lost.

Can we strike a balance between such uncompromising and antithetic changes?

9

PERSPECTIVE FOR TRIBAL DEVELOPMENT

Pandit Jawaharlal Nehru often used to say that 'planning is a continuous process'. He also had a fascination for the tribal people of India and was emotionally involved in their life, culture, problems and development. With his association with persons like Dr. Verrier Elwin, Dr. Behram Mehta, Prof. Christoph von-Furer Haimendorf and many others he could stimulate a process of social engineering and socio-cultural and economic changes in the tribal life. We have had a quick review of the strategies and the efforts in the direction since the beginning. Things have been done and goods delivered but much remains to be done. Experimentation with new schemes goes an continually and new structures or sub-structures are evolved and new dimensions are added to the existing ones. It will be worthwhile to acquaint ourselves with some latest innovations in plans and policies and also the fresh thinking on the launching of the Eighth Five-Year Plan, before concluding this monograph.

The Action Plan

The so-called special 'action plan' has been started for this area with accent on development. In fact this was prompted due to the increasing Naxalite activity gaining popular support. This, probably prompted the administration to introspect its own action which probably resulted in the action plan. Among other projects, it has accelerated the communication and irrigation schemes and rural electrification. In February 1991, the Chief Minister of Maharashtra stated in a public speech at Gadchiroli that the coverage under rural electrification which was earlier sixteen per cent has gone up to 84 per cent since the launching of the action plan. Huge funds which are being pumped-in on development plans include irrigation agriculture, education, health and communication.

The State Government has prepared Special Action Plans for the Gadchiroli and Chandrapur districts which include construction of roads, rural electrification, education, animal husbandry, cottage industries etc. It also includes creation of proper communication and rapport between the administration and the tribal community.

Special Action Plan for Gadchiroli District

In this district there are 1,491 towns/villages out of which only 678 are connected by roads. Out of the total roads total 45.6 per cent are tarred roads. Communication is hampered during rainy season and in some parts up to January for want of bridges and/or all season roads. Hence the Special Action Plan gives priority to road construction between 1991 to 2000 A.D. along with bridges. The target for the first 3-4 years are:

No. of Roads	–	97
Length of Additional Roads	–	1,338 km
Tarring	–	51 km
Cross Drainage Works	–	45
Small Bridges	–	217
Big Bridges	–	27

The proposed expenditure on these works is Rs. 39.05 crores.

Out of 1,491 villages/towns only 594 had been electrified till 1988. Out of the remaining 897 villages, permission from the Central Government under Forest Conservation Act is necessary for 296 villages, which is being expedited. But electrification will be taken-up speedily in the rest of the 601 villages for which such permission is not necessary. Solar energy based lights will be installed in some villages.

Rural health services will be widened by providing a Primary Health Centre (PHC) (or a Mobile Unit) in such a manner that every village will have it within a distance of 5-7 km. Buildings and staff quarters will also be provided to all centres. Primary as well as secondary schools with vocational education will also be increased: Nine new Ashram Schools will also be added — three in Etapalli tahsil, two in Aheri tahsil, three in Chamarshi and one in Dhanora tahsil. Percentage of literacy is extremely low, i.e. 24.58 per cent in the Gadchiroli district, and in Dhanora and Etapalli tahsils it is only 19.54 per cent and 10.39 per cent respectively (in Etapalli tahsil women's literacy is only 3.97 per cent). In view of this situation education will be given priority. Other priority area includes irrigation, horticulture, small and cottage industries, applied nutrition programme for pregnant women, nursing mothers and children up to six years of age.

The total outlay on special Action Plan for the Gadchiroli district is of about Rs. 135 crores. Details are given in Table 9.1.

TABLE 9.1 Details of Special Action Plan for Gadchiroli District

Sl. No.	Development Items	Details of Scheme	Approx. Expenditure (In Rupees Crores)
1.	Road Development	97 works 1,338 km Roads 45 cross water drainage 217 small bridges	39.05
2.	Rural Electrification	601 villages	62.00
3.	Public Health	19 Primary Health Centres 7 Public Health Centres	10.87
4.	Educational Development	26 + 248 schools, 400 teachers etc.	5.31
5.	Vocational Education	Upgrading of industrial institutes, Vocation education in schools	1.39
6.	Irrigation	16 small, 110 *pucca*, Bundhs 1683 open wells, 50 tubewells, etc.	8.43
7.	Horticulture	Mango, Cashewnut plantation	1.25
8.	Nutrition	Under I.C.D.S.	2.00
9.	Small Industry	Small and Cottage, Silk	1.00
10.	Buildings	For Police, Government Staff	3.00
		Total Rs.	134.30

Source: Information Book-let, Govt. of Maharashtra.

Revamping the planning machinery and continuous evaluation to see that those who were meant to receive the benefits did get them is also emphasised under the Special Action Plan. Necessary facilities like special jeep cars with driver have also been provided for the purpose. On the spot inspection of the development works —

particularly in the areas where Naxalites are active, has also been specifically mentioned in the draft of the scheme for the Gadchiroli district.

These additional funds, more facilities, revamping of the machinery and all efforts for expediting the development work indicates that the Government has tacitly accepted that the Tribal Sub-plan schemes did nto operate to their expectation and this also underlines a realisation that an honest prompt and foolproof implementation of the plan can thwart the terrorist activities from getting root and support in tribal areas.

People's Forest Policy Stressed[1]

The South Chandrapur Division of the Chandrapur Forest Division includes the primitive tribes area of Etapalli tahsil and the Aheri, Sironcha tahsils which are all tribal population dominated areas with Naxalite problem. This Division organised a workshop on, 'New Trends in Forest Protection — People's Participation', during February 1991, in which young, enthusiastic, I.F.S. trained forest officers participated. Shri Sunil Mitra, Conservator for South Chandrapur Division (the host division) regretted that Special Action Plan of the State Government, ironically enough, did no allot any funds to the Forest Department to which belongs 82 per cent of the land in the Gadchiroli district.

A very pertinent point was made by Shri Mitra when he said that in view of the Naxalite activities and the consequent intimidation and demoralisation of the staff of the Department, the customary regulatory role of the Forest Department is not going to be adequate. The protection of forests, he continued, is not merely a job of policing, and therefore the role of forest officers needs to be changed from a regulatory one to that of a development agency. It may be noted here that this has already been recommended in this book under chapter 5 (pp. 131, 132). Example of a Divisional Forest Officer who did attempt such schemes with quite a good success has also been given in this book (Also see Appendix V for details).

The Divisional Commissioner urged the Forest Officers to work out the form and pattern in which the forest inhabitants could participate in the forest production. So far they have been suspicious and cynical due to what had been going on so far and as such he stressed the need to convince them of the genuineness of the department's intentions. It was also necessary to see that no additional burden is brought upon them and that they are not denied the privileges and facilities which were enjoyed by them in the pest. Urging the Government to bear such burden the Commissioner also emphasised that the forest officers should develop the skill of communication with the tribals.

A question was raised as to whether the forests were needed to fulfil the needs of the people or to maintain the ecological balance? The rotation cycle of a tree was of forty years. In 1984 a Government report stated that at least one crore trees have to be felled every day (in 1984) to meet the then requirements of fuelwood fodder, paper, furniture construction etc. The figure was around fifteen lakhs trees per day for Maharashtra. These figures were quoted by Shri R.M. Sharma, Regional Manager of the Forest Development Corporation of Maharashtra (North Circle). The Deputy Conservator of Forests of Bhamragad Division informed that the wood cut by the tribals/or collected by, them for domestic purposes or as fuel wood is actually sold out for huge amount bringing a loss for the forest department. (His observations were based mainly on the Dahanu area of Thane district of Maharashtra and not the Gadchiroli district.) He quoted an example in which a tribal constructs a house using teak valued at the prevailing price up to Rs. 50,000 to Rs. 75,000. Unaware of this cost, he sells the house to outside traders and contractors for around Rs. 10,000 and then builds another house. Even the so-called fuel-wood sold out in cities every day is worth around Rs. 20 to Rs. 25 thousands.

The Problem of Boundaries

In the Chandrapur and Gadchiroli districts the villagers have no idea of the boundaries of protected forests and keep on encroaching. In the workshop it was pointed out that the forest land has not been fully and properly surveyed, demarcated and settled. The officers had long back submitted their survey reports regarding the settlement of traditional 'nistar' rights and other concessions to the tribals, however, the Government has not yet issued formal notification. In fact the tragedy is, that the boundaries of the protected and (formerly) ex-proprietary forests have not been properly demarcated. "*Pattas*" distributed in the past have also not been marked out properly. A large number of villages are still unsurveyed. As a result, many tribals really do not know the boundary of their fields and go on cultivating in the adjoining forest area. The Deputy Conservator of Forest, Sirondra Division, suggested the need for an immediate survey and demarcation (jointly by the Forest Department and Revenue Department and the District Inspector of Land Records). This problem of the settlement of the Revenue land *vis-a-vis* the forest land has been a chronic one which had even caused bitter litigation between the Revenue and the Forest Departments of the Maharashtra Government in 1973-74.[2] It was suggested at the workshop that

(i) with scientific forest management those forests that are not under the 'protected' category should be made more productive in terms of providing adequately for the traditional 'nistar' rights of tribals,
(ii) training be given to tribals in intensive agriculture, shifting of encroachments from the protected areas on an area exchange basis,
(iii) provision of hybridised cattle,
(iv) employment to landless labourers, and
(v) merger of smaller villages into bigger ones.

An experiment being tried in the Central Chandrapur Division was outlined by Shri Gairola, Deputy Conservator. Community participation was enlisted in protection of forest by taking into confidence and working out the total annual requirements of fuel-wood, bamboo and poles etc. in consultations with the tribal families. One member from each family will be enrolled (from three villages) as members of forest protection force. Initially the total forest area involved in this experiments will be 1600 hectares. Shri Gairola informed that 412 members have shown interest to participate in the scheme. An Executive Committee of nine, consisting of the Sarpanch, Up-sarpanch of those three villages with two beat guards and the round officer has been constituted. Four to six teak poles will be distributed free of charge to each member every year. These could be supplied from a stock of 9000 poles likely to be formed during the thinning operation every year. The members of this committee will also be engaged in the plantation on the 30 hectares of land for a period of ten years and will be paid 10 per cent of the wages as supervision charges. The total employment generation will be to the tune of sixty man-days every day, throughout the year. This scheme which is under consideration at State level for Statewide application may go a long way in motivating the villagers themselves to protect the forests.

Regarding encroachments and their eviction the participants felt that the villagers are willing to relieve their possession of their lands. The above scheme could be linked with the eviction from the large scale encroachments. But even this work has been hampered due to the extremely pathetic position of survey settlement and demarcation.

The Role of the Forest Officer

In the 1970s, forest villages were converted to revenue villages, breaking a host of relationship between the locals and forest officers and shrinking the officers' role to the managing and protecting an 'open treasure' with only two basic duties viz. that of an employer with limited resources and of primarily policing without adequate infrastructure to match it. 'Nistar' rights could not be fulfilled due to limited stocks and as the genuine demands of local people increased, any efforts to restrict and control removal of forest produce made the forest officer 'anti-public'. Giving vent to these facts the Deputy Conservator (Gadchiroli) of Forest pleaded for a developmental role for forest officers, even for the supply of 'Nistar' products and their alternatives and its effective utilisation.

Perspectives for Tribal Development during the Eighth Five Year Plan[3]

The need of orientation of the approach and policy for tribal development has been emphasised in the approach paper to the Eighth Five Year Plan, by the Planning Commission and the National Development Council. The Eighth Plan running from 1990-1995 is supposed to take care of the following points which are a feed-back from the evaluation and experience of the earlier years.

(1) The Scheduled Tribe population is getting eroded, through a combination of development interventions, commercial exploi- tation and ineffective legal and administrative systems. The trend needs to be arrested, as it can undermine the very survival of these communities.

(2) The big projects in irrigation, power and transport often disrupt the life and environment of large number of Scheduled Tribe families, and the benefits mainly accrue to the populations in the plains. The relief and the rehabilitation measures are neither adequate nor property implemented.
(3) So as to ensure that the lives of the Scheduled Tribes are not disrupted in the name of national progress, programmes need to be deviced with the involvement of the Scheduled Tribes themselves in the light of their own order of priorities to remove economic, educational and social disparities to which they are subject.
(4) They should have access to minimum social services.
(5) Assistance in scientific resource conservation should be given.
(6) Construction of small water harvesting and storage system.
(7) Restoration of their traditional rights to forest produce and direct links with market.
(8) Strengthening of their traditional community organisations.

Workable Suggestions for Development Strategy during Eighth Plan

The Planning Commission formed professional groups for the formulation of the strategy for the Eighth Five Year Plan. The Socio-economic group on Welfare and Development of Scheduled Tribes made the following recommendations and suggestions to be considered while formulating the schemes for Tribal Development.

1. The Central Advisory Council for Harijans and Scheduled Tribes which were in existence till above April 1960 should be revived.
2. The report of the committee on programmes under poverty allevation should be implemented.
3. Centrally-sponsored schemes meant for Scheduled Tribes should not be transferred to the State.
4. There was need for unified administrative structure in the tribal areas.
5. Integrated system of health services and use of mobile dispensaries should be provided to the tribal areas.
6. Traditional Tribal Institutions and their community spirit should be used by tackling developmental problems of tribal

areas and managing their own affairs.

7. The autonomy of tribal villages should be ensured and the District and Village Councils should play an important role.
8. Autonomous District Councils may not be as effective as autonomous village councils.
9. Panchayati Raj system will not work for the benefit of Scheduled Castes and Scheduled Tribes, unless these bodies are wholly composed of S.C.s/S.T.s.
10. Voluntary and social service organisations of non-political character should be involved in promoting developmental activities.
11. The working of the Scheduled Tribes Development Corporation needs toning up.
12. All-weather roads in tribal areas is a necessity.
13. Employment programmes should be linked with local resources.
14. Minor Forest Produce prices commission be set-up.
15. There was enough scope to improve the economy of tribal people through collection, processing and marketing of minor forest produce and particularly the medicinal plants.
16. Land must be considered as a basic resource of the tribals.
17. Country liquor shops in the tribal areas should be closed down.
18. Endeavour should be made to wean the tribals from drinking.
19. Consumption of liquor by personnel serving in tribal areas should be prohibited.
20. Right to life should be protected, which meant command over resources.
21. Exploitation should be tackled on a priority basis.
22. Educational development should be accorded highest priority.
23. Universities should be involved in a more effective manner in the programmes of Ministry of Welfare to train S.C./S.T. candidates for entrance examinations.
24. Drop-outs at primary level is a serious problem and remedial measure should be taken to tackle it.
25. The norms of setting-up Adult Education Centre were too unrealistic, and did not take into account the varying socio-economic groups within the tribes, and hence need revision.
26. Special attention should be paid to small primitive tribal groups numbering about 74.

Apart from the above recommendations and suggestions, there seemed to be a consensus on certain points among members like the wastage and pilferage of expenditure, the need to recognise the ethnic pride and cultural identity of tribals and the problem of exploitation of tribals *vis-a-vis* the growth and spread of terrorist (e.g. Naxalite) activities in tribal areas. The author (who was also a Member of this professional group on S.T.s) has seen and said that it was exploitation of tribals that breeds extremism. Dr. B.D. Sharma, Commissioner, S.C./S.T.s also opined that the Naxalite problem in the tribal areas is a direct consequence of not redressing the legitimate grievances of the tribal people.

The documents briefly reviewed above show that there is a lot of awareness at the planning level as well at the highest executive echelons regarding the maladies, pathos and problems. Even the solutions are ready for trial. What remains is the political will and an army of intelligent, non-corrupt and dedicated officers with similar support from the voluntary social organisation/workers. It will be appropriate to quote Shri V.R. Krishna Iyer, Former Judge Supreme Court of India, as it will be a benefiting conclusion to what has been discussed in this book. Shri Iyer says, "The Fourth World within the Third World — the Tribal People — will never surrender until the Preamble to the Constitution fulfils itself. They demand militant social and economic justice. They fight for equality in every dimension. They scoff at the fraud of progress which denies to them fraternity and human dignity. Therefore, the future of our country must be fashioned by new strategies of integration of the tribal population sans which there can never be justice in the authentic sense".[4]

NOTES

1. *The Hitarada*, English Daily, Nagpur — Report of Workshop on the issued dated the 28th Feb. and 1st & 3rd March, 1991
2. Deogaonkar, S.G., 1982, *The Media of Bhamragad*, Inter India Pub., New Delhi, p. 72.
3. Planning Commission, *Approach to the Eighth Five Year Plan (1990-95)*, GOI, New, Delhi, May 1990, pp. 31-32.
4. Deogaonkar, S.G, *Tribal Exploitation*, Inter-India Publications, New Delhi, 1990, p. 7.

APPENDICES

APPENDIX I

List of Beneficiaries and the Benefits Studied

All these Beneficiaries were actually contacted, verifications made and their reactions ascertained

Sl. No.	Name of the Beneficiary	The Benefit	Year	Agency	Remarks
1.	2.	3.	4.	5.	6.
(I) Aldandi					
1.	Modi Vadde Parsa	Pair of Bullocks	85-86	T.D.C.	
2.	Karve Keye Metami	Pair of Bullocks	85-86	T.D.C.	
3.	Buklu Bandu Madkami	Tiles for roof	84-85	S.C.A.	
4.	Modi Pusu Metami	-do-	-do-	-do-	
5.	Chinna Penda Atlami	-do-	-do-	-do-	
6.	Pusu Karpa Pungati	-do-	-do-	-do-	
7.	Chamru Adwe	-do-	-do-	-do-	
8.	Soma Dasru Vidapi	Pair of Bullocks and Bullock cart	-do-	-do-	
9.	Pusu Adwe Metami	-do-	-do-	-do-	
(II) Arewada					
10.	Fakri Vijja Gawade	Tiles for Roof	84-85	P.O.	
11.	Menga Banda Kulmeti	-do-	-do-	-do-	
12.	Pusu Iriya Kulmeti	-do-	-do-	-do-	
13.	Kumma Irpa Gota	-do-	-do-	-do-	
14.	Shankar Vistari Kumre	Brick-making (Rs. 2000)	85-86	T.D.C.	(Not recd. by bene.)
15.	Mulla Maddi Hidami	Pair of Bullocks	84-85	T.D.C.	IRDP.
16.	Poriya Maddi Hidami	-do-	-do-	-do-	
17.	Kana Kopa Pungati	Bullock cart.	-do-	-do	
18.	Prabhakar Linga Kumre	-do-	-do-	-do-	
19.	Pusu Vadde Hidami	-do-	-do-	-do-	

Contd.

1.	2.	3.	4.	5.	6.
(III)	**Bhamragad (Tola)**				
20.	Smt. Sumitra Govinda Talande	Sewing Machine (Rs. 1500)	84-85	T.D.C.	
21.	Narayan Warlu Madavi	-do-	81-82	T.D.C.	
22.	Keshav Chinna Madavi	Cycle-shop (Rs. 2500)	84-85	T.D.C.	Opened at Tadgaon.
23.	Mangru Chaitu Madavi	Pair of bullocks.	84-85	T.D.C.	Not recd. a yet
24.	Prabhakar Govinda Talande	Bullock-cart	85-86	T.D.C.	N.B.
25.	Vaman Lachmaji Uike	Grocery-shop (Rs.5000) (Rs. 2500 received)	85-86	T.D.C.	Shop not started.
26.	Ramsha Koksha Madavi	Oil engine	82-83	T.D.O.	Given as hires.
27.	Mangru Chaitu Gota (Madavi)	Training in animal husbandry- 1 month. stipend Rs. 300 Received one cow one calf, six goats	82-83	D.A.H.O.	
28.	Malu Keye Poladi	-do-	82-83	--do--	
29.	Laxman Mengji Veladi	Vegetable shop (Rs.1000).	85-86	T.D.C.	Has not opened shop.
30.	Dunga Irpa Gumma. (President, Fishermens' Co-op. Society, Bhamragad.).	(i) Earthwork implements. (Iron pan, spade, crow-bar, pick-axe).	85-86	D.F.O.	Recd.from D.F.O.
		(ii) Tiles for roof.	85-86	P.O.	
		(iii) Fish-seed spread in lakes.	84-85	P.O.	
		(iv) Two ferry boats were to be handed over to his society within a week.	86-87	P.O.	
31.	Maroti Mutta Madavi	Hut-repairs-i.e. Tiles for roofing given	84-85	P.O.	Bhamragad.
32.	Ganesh Jalamsha Atram	Earth work emplements	82-83	D.F.O.	

Contd.

1.	2.	3.	4.	5.	6.
(IV)	**Bangadi**				
33.	Gudsa Dura Parsa	(i) Tiles for roof	84-85	P.O.	
		(ii) Trip to Nagpur and other places	86-87	P.O.	
(V)	**Binagunda**				
34.	Sayabi Kana Durva (Gayata)	Oil engine, pair of Bullocks Bullocks cart. Alluminium & Brass utensils.	86-87	T.D.O. P.O.	Between 1982-83 to 83-84
35.	Nenda Suku Parsa	Animal Husbandry	86-87	D.A.H.O.	
36.	Samru Mura Timma.	training-1 month Rs. 300 stipend. cow yet to be received (25-4-87).	86-87	D.A.H.O.	
37.	Chukku Saitu Durva	Trip to Nagpur etc.	86-87	P.O.	(N.B.)
38.	Gogga Watte Durva	Trip to Nagpur etc.	86-87	P.O.	
39.	Doba Masa Parsa	Trip to Nagpur etc.	86-87	P.O.	
(VI)	**Bodange**				
40.	Kohla Gudsa Pungati	Pair of bullocks.	84-85	S.C.A.	
41.	Mahru Jivva Pungati	Pair of bullocks.	84-85	S.C.A.	
42.	Dunge Oka Pungati	Bullock-cart.	85-86		(N.B.)
(VII)	**Dhodraj**				
43.	Bande Budga Mohanda	Bullocks & cart cow/Milk Kettle.	85-86	I.T.D.P.	P.O.
44.	Smt. Povari Masa Kovasa	Rs. 500 for Broom purchase	84-85	M.S.T.D.C.	She never applied nor recd. amount.
45.	Smt. Rukmabai Gosai Sedam.	Oil engine.	84-85	T.D.O.	In good use.
46.	Kehaka Chuku Pungati	Ploughing of 5 acres by tractor Bullocks + cart.	85-86	P.O.(N.B.)	

Contd.

1.	2.	3.	4.	5.	6.
47.	Soma Bande Kursami	Tiles for (400 + 30)	85-86		Dissolved with first rain.
		2 acres of land ploughed by tractor			No ploughing due to hardness. Traditional tractor used.
48.	Poriya Chuku Mohanda	Animal Husbandry training-stipend for one month Rs.300 one cow+ calf + one she goat; Kettle.	85-86	Dy. Dir. A.H.D.	The cow died after one month
49.	Maguru Maida Michhya	Utensils for family welfare			
50.	Kolhu Chuku Kursami	Animal Husbandry training- Cow etc. & Kettles.	85-86.	Dy. Dir. A.H.D.	
51.	Vijja Kariya Majji	—do—	-do-	-do-	
52.	Chinna Doge Kudiyami	—do—	-do-	—do-	
53.	Chaitu Paika Pungati	—do—	-do-	—do-	
54.	Pandu Murra Gota	Tiles for roofing.	84-85		
55.	Soma Gilla Mohanda	—do—	84-85		
56.	Pusu Chuku Pungati	—do—	84-85		
57.	Vijja Tarya Pusali	—do—	84-85		
(VIII) Gongwada					
58.	Kana Pusu Pungati	Pair of bullocks	86-87	P.O.	
59.	Kopa Modyami	Cart only	86-87	P.O.	Signed but did not bring it.
60.	Doge Konda Modyami	Cart only	84-85		—
61.	Malu Kopa Modyami	Tiles for roof.	84-85		Taken by other man Chaitu Gilla Pungati.
62.	Gudru Doba Pallo	Pair of Bullocks.	84-85.		

Contd.

1.	2.	3.	4.	5.	6.
(IX)	**Gotpadi**				
63.	Pusu Karpa Varse	Pair of bullocks	84-85		
64.	Gogga Kohla Pungati	Bullock-cart	85-86		Actually he got it in 87 has old parts.
65.	Kumma Vale Pungati (His son Ulge was interviewed Kumma is dead	Bullock cart.	85-86		'As per list Benefit was actually given in April 1987 after the man died.
66.	Pusu Karpa Varse.	Pair of bullocks	84-85		got after one year. i.e. during 86.
67.	D.J. Warwade	Teacher at Gotpadi Primary School. (Training in Madia dialect).	85-86 & 86-87		
(X)	**Gundenhod**				
68.	Vatte Kotla Vadde	Tiles for roof Bullocks + cart Oil engine.	83-84 84-85 84-85.		(Engine in use).
69.	Karya Vatte Pungati.	Pair of bullocks.	84-85		(One bullock died)
70.	Bande Saitu Parsa	Tiles for roofing	83-84		
71.	Masa Vijja Durva	Tiles for roof. Pair of bullocks.	83-84. 84-85.		
72.	Maharu Chaito Pallo	Pair of bullocks	84-85		(On 100% subsidy).
(XI)	**Hemalkasa**				
73.	Lok-Biradari Prakalpa	As per Table attached	1982-83 84-85 85-86 86-87.	P.O., I.T.D.P.	

Contd.

1.	2.	3.	4.	5.	6.
74.	Bandu Korke Vadde	Bullock cart	85-86	I.T.D.P.	
		Tiles for roof.	84-85	I.T.D.P.	
	(his son Raju Korke (Vadde).	One acre field ploughed by tractor.	85-86.	I.T.D.P.	
75.	Bandu Korke Vadde	Ploughing by tractor Tiles for roof. (Chaityu Korke Pallos' Tiles taken by him as former has left the village.	85-86	I.T.D.P.	
76.	Hurra Vittha Telami	Land ploughed by tractor.	85-86.	I.T.D.P.	
(XII)	**Hiddur**	(All of them told that they got tiles only after they got operated for Family Planning.).			
77.	Zuru Boge Pungati	Tiles for roofing.	86-87	P.O.,	I.T.D.P.
78.	Koriya Dunga Durva.	--do-- Bullock-cart. Repairs to hut. (i.e. tiles).	84-85	S.C.A.	
79.	Biccha Keya Gota.	Tiles.	85-86.		I.T.D.P.
80.	Jogi Boge Pungati.	-do-	84-85		I.T.D.P.
81.	Mura Masa Timma	-do-	85-86		I.T.D.P.
82.	Gatti Bodanga Naroti	-do-	85-86		I.T.D.P.
83.	Ghaitu Keye Alami	-do-	85-86		I.T.D.P.
84.	Katia Poriya Vidpi	-do-	85-86		I.T.D.P.
85.	Soma Kurka Veladi	-do-	85-86		I.T.D.P.
86.	Jogi Bonge Pungati	-do-	85-86		I.T.D.P.
87.	Rama Vijja Parsu	-do-	85-86		I.T.D.P.
88.	Komti Narango Madkami	-do-	85-86		I.T.D.P
(XIII)	**Hitapadi**				
			P.O.		
89.	Rainu Narango Pungati.	Tiles for roof.	84-85	I.T.D.P.	After F.P. operation.
90.	Jola Bichha Timma	-do-	-do-	-do-	-do-
91.	Povari Narango	-do-	-do-	-do-	got operated but did not get tiles.

Contd.

1.	2.	3.	4.	5.	6.
92.	Karve Narango Pungati	Pair of bullocks and cart.	85-86	T.D.C.	He wants imple-ment for black smi-thy and tiles.
(XIV)	**Juvvi**				
93.	Suku Kumma Pusali.	Bullocks and cart. 85-86	84-85	P.O. I.T.D.P.	100% subsidy.
94.	Pusu Geba Pungati.	Tiles	84-85	P.O. I.T.D.P.	
		Animal Husbandry training. A cow & a calf. Milk-can, Cycle.	86-87 86-87 March 87.	I.T.D.P.	Refused bullock cart from Forest Deptt. as its was not of good quality (i.e. what he says).
95.	Rama Geba Pungati	Tiles Milk-can	86-87	I.T.D.P.	50% sub-sidy basis.
96.	Vijja Dasca Pungati-	Milk-can Cycle	86-87		
(XV)	**Kiyar**				
97.	Bandu Vanga Madavi Teacher	Metal-work training	82-83	I.T.D.P.	
98.	Guna Peka Kudyeti	Oil engine.	83-84	I.T.D.P.	Not in use.
99.	Arsu Rama Pungati	Pair of bullocks.	85-86	S.C.A.	
100.	Mahari Boti Pungati	Tiles.	85-86		After F.P. opera-tion).
101.	Smt. Gomi Pandhra	-do-	85-86		-do-
102.	Dasru Doge Pungati	-do-	-do-		-do-
103.	Gunna Peka Kudyeti-	-do-	-do-		-do-
(XVI)	**Koyar**				
104.	Goga Ulga Pungati	Bullocks & cart/ Tiles.	84-85	P.O., I.T.D.P.	

Contd.

1.	2.	3.	4.	5.	6.
105.	Dogai Doba Pungati	-do--	84-85	I.T.D.P.	
106.	Sayabi Bande Pallo	-do-	-do-	I.T.D.P.	
107.	Ghaitu Budga Pungati	Only Bullocks	85-86		
(XVII) Kuvvakodi					
108.	Edma Banga Usendi	Utensils/Blanket (& all other houses) Renewal of Patelship.	86-87	I.T.D.P.	Discussed with S.D.O.
109.	Mura Banga Usendi & wife Kotla Mesa Parsa (of Binagunda).	Marriage expendi- ture.	84-85	I.T.D.P.	
110.	Raju Soma Usendi.	Animal Husbandry Trg. cow, calf + one Bull. Milk-can (cycle to be received).	Feb.87.	I.T.D.P.	
111.	Kumma Suku Usendi	—do—	Feb. 87.	I.T.D.P.	
112.	Namdeo Rama Usendi	Pair of Bu llocks.	84-85	I.T.D.P.	
113.	Gogga Vanga Usendi	—do—	-do-	I.T.D.P.	
114.	Irpa Gudsa Usendi	—do—	-do-	I.T.D.P.	
115.	Bodanga Keye Usendi	—do—	-do-	I.T.D.P.	
116.	Hara Singa Kalanga	Tiles for roof	85-86	I.T.D.P.	
117.	Ku. Gamme Usendi	Trip to Nagpur	86-87	I.T.D.P.	
118.	Ku. Masri Suku Usendi	—do—	86-87	I.T.D.P.	
(XVIII) Laheri					
119.	Narango Pusu Naroti	4 cycles for hire-shop.	84-85	T.D.C.	
120.	Rama Pandu Timma	Animal Husbandry Training.stipend and cow.	86-87.	Dy. Dir. A.H.	
121.	Keye Fakri Vadde.	—do—	86-87	-do-	
122.	Kariya Bandu Madkami	—do—	-do-	-do-	
123.	Vatte Mulla Kudyami	—do—	-do-	-do-	
124.	Kumma Dasru Vadde	Tiles for roof.	84-85	T.D.C.	
125.	Doge Ulge Kudyami	—do—	-do-	-do-	
126.	Korke Vanja Gota	(Prakashtha Upkarane) earth work implements, pick-axe) (crow-bar, iron-pan, spade)	85-86	D.F.O.	

Contd.

1.	2.	3.	4.	5.	6.
127.	Narango Pusu Naroti	—do—	85-86	-do-	
128.	Dasru Doge Kudyemi	—do—	-do-	-do-	
129.	Vatte Sonya Atram	Pair of bullocks	84-85	P.O., I.T.D.P.	
		Bullock-cart	85-86	-do-	UPTO April 87 he had not received higher of the two Notice was received for repayment of loan on these two items.
130.	Hevda Adwe Bogami.	Oil engine. used on well (ground-nut plot).	85-86	T.D.O.	
131.	Kumma Koti Bogami	Oil engine used on Nulla-(ground-nut plot).	84-85	T.D.O.	
132.	Dugga Gogga Vadde.	Oil engine. used on well.	85-86	T.D.O.	Vegetable plantation-chilli, brinjals etc.

(XIX) **Malampoddur**

1.	2.	3.	4.	5.	6.
133.	Kum. Nirmala Sitaram Sadmek.	Anganwadi worker.			Interview.
134.	Raju Chaitu Pungati.	Animal Hus Trg. cow and cycle.	85-86	P.O., I.T.D.P.	
135.	Suku Mura Durva	—do—	-do-	I.T.D.P.	
136.	Zuru Pedu Pallo	—do—	-do-	I.T.D.P.	Did not receive cow.
137.	Rama Gara Vadde	—do—	-do-	I.T.D.P.	—do—
138.	Zuru Poriya Durva	—do—	-do-	I.T.D.P.	—do—
139.	Lacchu Kotla Vadde	—do—	-do-	I.T.D.P.	—do—
140.	Lacchu Mangru Kursami	—do—	-do-	I.T.D.P.	—do—
141.	Malu Pusu Vadde	Tiles for roof	85-86(N.B.)		

Contd.

1.	2.	3.	4.	5.	6.
142.	Bandu Masa Vadde	Repair to hut	-do-		"Got tiles only
143.	Kolu Gutha Vachami	Bullocks & cart.	84-85 85-86	P.O.I.T.D.P.	
144.	Malu Pusu Durethi.	Pair of Bullocks.	84-85	-do-	
145.	Smt. Chene Pusu Vadde	—do—	84-85	-do-	
	(XX) Murangal				
146.	Bodi Darsa Vadde	Pair of bullocks.	85-86	-do-	
147.	Tugge Aara Pungati	Pair of bullocks and cart.	84-85	-do-	
148.	Kana Baya Pallo	—do—	84-85	-do-	
149.	Dogai Desa Vadde	Cart only	83-84	-do-	
150.	Poriya Irpa Pungati	Tiles for roof	85-86	-do-	
151.	Chaitu Doli Pungati	—do—	85-86	-do-	
	(XXI) Nelgunda				
152.	Sayabi Dassa Varse	Bullock-cart	85-86	-do-	(without tyres, hence did not accept it, but signature given).
153.	Dasru Goha Mahka	Bullocks	84-85	-do-	
154.	Poriya Irpa Mahka	—do—	-do-	-do-	
155.	Gota Musra Mohanda	—do—	-do-	-do-	
156.	Jimo Chaitu Maharu	Tiles for roof	-do-	-do-	
157.	Bhiva Madgu Atram	Oil engine	82-83	-do-	
	(XXII) Turremarka				
158.	Pege Bura Pungati	Pair of bullocks	84-85	T.D.C.	
159.	Kana Patru Velati	—do—	-do-	-do-	
160.	Vadde Gudsa Vadde	—do—	-do-	-do-	
161.	Daggu Kumbha Podati	—do—	-do-	-do-	
162.	Mangru Irpa Podati	—do—	-do-	-do-	
163.	Badde Murra Podati	Goat keeping (Rs. 2000).	84-85	-do-	

From I.T.D.P. (Etapalli)

Sr. No.	Name of the Beneficiary	The Benefit	Year	Agency	Remarks
1.	2.	3.	4.	5.	6.
(I)	**Chokhewada**				
1.	Rayaji Nanu Matami	Gobar-gas plant.	85-86	P.S.	Out of order, wrongly constructed.
2.	Janglee Mahajan Usendi	—do—	-do-	-do-	Out of order.
3.	Rainu Madari Madavi	—do—	-do-	-do-	In use for cooking.
4.	Yesu Danu Naroti	—do—	-do-	-do-	—do—
5.	Nevru Gundri Gota	—do—	-do-	-do-	—do—
6.	Desru Navlu Hodi (500+30)	Tiles for roofing	85-86	P.O.(N.B.)	obtained and used seen on roofs.
7.	Kala Lalsa Padko	—do—	-do-	—do—	—do—
8.	Smt. Mili Tanu Matami	-do—	-do-	-do-	—do—
9.	Yesu Tiru Gota	-do-	-do-	-do-	—do—
10.	Rayaj Tanu Matami	-do-	-do-	-do-	—do—
11.	Manku Ganu Matami	Training in English Typing (30 W.P.M.)	-do- (total benefit upto Rs. 190).	-do-	Trained and satisfied. Expects help for post-graduation after passing B.Com. Exam.
12.	Mangru Devu Naroti (Perma and local social worker.)	—	—	—	He demanded drinking water well for the village.

Contd.

1.	2.	3.	4.	5.	6.
(II) Dumme					
13.	Patadi Pusu Pungati.	---do---	84-85	P.K.V.	Using it for earning
(III) Etapalli					
14.	Masu Gota Patel	—	—		Ex-Chairman, Panchayat Samiti, Etapalli.
(IV) Geda					
15.	Danu Katiya Pada.	Electric-pump.		T.D.O.	Out of use.
(V) Jarawandi					
16.	Laxman Mahadeo Kodape.	For General Stores (Rs. 5,000).	85-86	T.D.C.	Not started keeps articles in his old Pan shop
17.	Harishchandra Lahuji Madavi	----do----	-do--	-do-	Started store at Kosansur.
18.	Prabhakar Saoji Meshram.	For Maneri shop.	-do-	-do-	Not stared
19.	Smt. Jamunabai Dattu Madavi.	Sewing Machine. (Rs. 1500).	-do-	-do-	Using the machine and earning livelihood.
20.	Namdeo Subhan Madavi	----do----	-do--	-do-	--do---
21.	Bhanudas Zingruji Madvai.	For Goat keeping (Rs. 2,000).	-do--	-do-	Did not collect as he was not informed.

Contd.

1.	2.	3.	4.	5.	6.
(VI)	**Javelli**				
22.	Girma Sitaram Meshram	Gobar-Gas plant	83-84	P.S.	Plant Thrust upon him—he has no cattle to feed Go-bar gas plant. Out of order.
23.	Bichanga Durga Talandi	—do—	84-85	-do-	—do—
24.	Namdeo Musli Atram.	Sewing Machine	83-84	P.K.V.	Being used for earning livelihood.
25.	Bajrao Soma Sidam. (Javelli)	Sewing machine	P.K.V. 83-84		Being used for earning livelihood.
(VII)	**Kandhli**				
26.	Bisan Arjun Madavi.	Vegetable shop (Rs. 1,000).	85-86	T.D.C.	Received Rs. 500 as 1st Instal-ment but did not start the shop.
27.	Gomaji Maharu Madavi	Tiles for roofing (600+30 tiles).	85-86	T.D.C.	Got the tiles.
28.	Saoji Chinna Madvai	—do—	-do-	-do—	—do—
29.	Smt. Yamabai Warlu Kodape.	—do—	-do-	-do-	—do—
30.	Lalsu Kisan Tekam	—do—	-do-	-do-	—do—
31.	Laxman Lahanu Tekam	—do—	-do-	-do-	—do—

Contd.

1.	2.	3.	4.	5.	6.
(VIII) Kasansur					
32.	Komti Devu Madavi	Oil Engine.	78-79	T.D.O.	In use with good results.
33.	Dasru Pati Hedo	--do--	80-81	--do--	--do--
34.	Raju Dolu Narotey	--do--	84-85	--do--	--do--
35.	Kotla Malu Pallo	For General Stores. (Rs. 5,000)	85-86	T.D.C.	He has nor collected the amount
36.	Manu Chaitu Pallo	For Poultry. (Rs. 2,000)	85-86	--do--	--do--
37.	Dasru Pati Hedo	Gobar-gas plant.	85-86	P.S.	Plant choked-up out of use.
(IX) Krishnar					
38.	Ganda Dolu Hichami	Oil engine.	82-83	T.D.O.	In order.
39.	Murra Karpa Talandi.	—do—	-do-	-do-	--do--
40.	Firangi Peka Kando	Gobar-gas plant	82-83	P.S.	Out of order.
41.	Mirwa Ganda Hichami	---do---	-do-	-do--	Out of order.
42.	Chaitu Murra Talandi	---do—	-do-	-do-	Out of order Subsidy not received. State Bank loan increasing
(X) Pandhevahi					
43.	Ghisu Irapa Atram	Gobar-gas plant.	84-85	P.S.	Out of order.

APPENDIX II

List of 31 Villages under I.T.D.P. (Primitive Tribe), Bhamragad

Sl. No.	Name of Village	Number of families	Population	S.T. Population
1.	Kuvakodi*	21	97	97
2.	Damanmarka	5	12	12
3.	Pungasur	3	11	11
4.	Pirmalbhatti	10	34	34
5.	Turemarka*	13	114	114
6.	Mordpar	11	51	51
7.	Fodewada	16	85	85
8.	Timeli	6	48	48
9.	Dirangi	2	8	8
10.	Korparai	5	27	27
11.	Binagunda*	20	106	106
12.	Tadpar	6	17	17
13.	Pusewada	7	39	39
14.	Murangal*	25	126	126
15.	Koyar*	7	40	40
16.	Poyarkothi	24	151	151
17.	Bangadi*	12	34	34
18.	Midadapalli	36	278	239
19.	Kawande	19	103	103
20.	Gundenhod*	6	38	38
21.	Gundurwahi	18	111	111
22.	Malenga	—	—	—
23.	Gardewada	—	—	—
24.	Hikameta	—	—	—
25.	Japeli	—	—	—
26.	Tulwada	—	—	—
27.	Kotwada	—	—	—
28.	Gunjun	—	—	—
29.	Vegurwada	—	—	—
30.	Fulcher	—	—	—
31.	Fulnar	—	—	—
	Total	272	1,523	1,484

Obtained from — Office of the Project Officer, I.T.D.P. Gadchiroli No. I, Bhamragad.

Note: 10 villages are deserted.

* These villages were selected for study.

APPENDIX III

List of Viliages of Primitives Tribes in Bhamragad Area

Sl. No.	Name of Village	Sl. No.	Name of Village
1.	Lashkar	30.	Bengadi*
2.	Hodari	31.	Bhusewada
3.	Gopanar	32.	Murangal*
4.	Hitapadi*	33.	Golaguda
5.	Haldandi*	34.	Bhatapar
6.	Moradpar	35.	Madapalli
7.	Hidur*	36.	Kawande
8.	Kathalasur	37.	Koyangunda
9.	Gundenhod*	38.	Juvvi*
10.	Timeli	39.	Darba
11.	Fodewada	40.	Dubbagoda
12.	Dirangi	41.	Midadapalli
13.	Mirguwancha	42.	Hitalwara
14.	Pidmili	43.	Gongwada*
15.	Nargunda	44.	Gotpadi*
16.	Halwer	45.	Bodange*
17.	Kumhur	46.	Kukkameta
18.	Padhur	47.	Kuvakodi*
19.	Dobur	48.	Permilbhatti
20.	Poyarkoti	49.	Pungasur
21.	Irapanar	50.	Malampodur*
22.	Gongawada*	51.	Laheri*
23.	Dhodraj*	52.	Tadapar
24.	Kucher	53.	Turemarka*
25.	Koyar*	54.	Damanmarka
26.	Gongawada	55.	Binagunda*
27.	Nelgunda*	56.	Muspadi
28.	Paraynar	57.	Hindewada
29.	Pusawara		

* These villages were selected for study.

APPENDIX IV

List of Villages covered Under R.C. (Revenue Circle) Bhamragad

(*Census 1981*)

Sl. No.	Census Code No. 1981	Name of Village	Population	No. of S.T.
1	2	3	4	5
1.	200	Arewada*	492	318
2.	269	Ranipodur	169	169
3.	252	Lashkar	175	171
4.	253	Hodri	162	162
5.	251	Hitapadi*	54	54
6.	212	Gopnar	137	137
7.	254	Haldandi (Aldandi)*	65	65
8.	206	Moradpar	51	51
9.	250	Hiddur*	133	126
10.	213	Kasansoor	50	49
11.	257	Gundenhod*	38	38
12.	207	Timeli (M)	41	41
13.	208	Fodewada (M)	85	85
14.	204	Dirangi	8	8
15.	205	Fulcher (M)	--	—
16.	266	Mallampodur*	377	275
17.	265	Laheri (S)*	669	554
18.	268	Kukkameta	275	187
19.	261	Kuvakodi*	97	97
20.	210	Pirmalbhatti	34	34
21.	262	Pungasoor	11	11
22.	258	Tadpar (M)	17	17
23.	209	Turremarka (M)*	114	52
24.	211	Damanmarka	12	12
25.	259	Binagunda (M)*	546	221
26.	264	Muspadi	16	16
27.	256	Laheri (M)	—	—
28.	260	Vegurwada (M)	—	—
29.	267	Hindewada (M)	200	198
30.	303	Bhamragad*	593	281
31.	382	Bhatpar	439	371
32.	320	Golaguda	295	293

(*Contd.*)

APPENDIX-IV (*Contd.*)

1	2	3	4	5
33.	305	Medpalli	229	226
34.	380	Kawande	103	103
35.	321	Koyanguda	127	127
36.	371	Darba	153	153
37.	383	Hitalwara	53	53
38.	304	Dubaguda	40	40
39.	379	Malenga	—	—
40.	319	Juvi*	121	120
41.	381	Midadapalli	278	239
42.	318	Ghotpadi*	53	53
43.	372	Bodange*	58	58
44.	378	Gundenur	—	—
45.	316	Garewada	—	—
46.	306	Dhodraj*	358	308
47.	307	Irpnar	161	158
48.	373	Gongawada (M)	—	—
49.	308	Kucher (M)	37	20
50.	309	Kokapadi	—	—
51.	311	Kotwada	—	—
52.	312	Koyar (M)*	40	40
53.	376	Gardewada	—	—
54.	374	Gongwada (S)*	283	281
55.	314	Japeli (M)	—	—
56.	313	Nulwara	—	—
57.	375	Nelgunda*	608	534
58.	317	Paraynar	338	328
59.	377	Puswara	39	39
60.	263	Bangadi*	34	34
61.	256	Bhusewada	65	65
62.	310	Murangal*	826	761
63.	315	Hikkameta	—	—
64.	300	Todgaon	302	227
65.	271	Karampalli	207	202
66.	272	Kumarguda	104	104
67.	323	Kehakapara	80	80
68.	322	Palli (S)	324	312
69.	220	Mardahur (S)	52	52
70.	302	Hemalkasa*	605	516
71.	245	Kodpe	24	24
72.	247	Tekala	141	141
73.	246	Tirkametta	59	59
74.	218	Pokur	70	70

(*Contd.*)

APPENDIX-IV (*Contd.*)

1	2	3	4	5
75.	301	Bejur	74	74
76.	219	Mutenwahi	—	—
77.	244	Kosfundi	217	156
78.	248	Kiyar (S)*	390	254
79.	249	Krishnar (S)	228	228
80.	199	Kothi (S)	519	493
81.	198	Padhur (S)	82	82
82.	215	Mirgulwancha	206	198
83.	197	Kumbur	—	—
84.	196	Kucher	64	64
85.	162	Korparsi	27	27
86.	195	Khandindiwadi	328	222
87.	201	Gundurwahi	111	111
88.	94	Dobhur	189	187
89.	217	Nargunda	222	211
90.	200	Pidmili	56	56
91.	202	Fulnar	—	—
92.	203	Poyarkothi	151	149
93.	156	Walavi	80	51
94.	116	Halwer	138	138
95.	298	Kudkeli	381	300
96.	326	Kedmara	313	197
97.	272	Dhulepalli	331	272
98.	274	Botanfundi	205	196
99.	242	Wateli	196	195
100.	226	Visamundi	355	336
101.	222	Visamundi (Gundapuri) (M)	106	100
102.	223	Gundapuri	78	78
103.	239	Fundi	3	3
104.	243	Venganur	83	46
105.	366	Chichoda	294	291
106.	367	Jinjgaon	354	333
107.	369	Kasansoor	141	140
108.	334	Padampalli	107	107
109.	368	Boriya	147	147
110.	299	Irakdumme (M)	132	129
111.	325	Kedmara (M)	—	—
112.	365	Gornur (M)	110	110
113.	370	Zareguda (M)	16	16
Total			17,761	15,317

List Supplied by: I.T.D.P. Gadchiroli No. I, Bhamragad.
Total inhabited (M) villages — 17.
Total villages with habitation — 96.
* Selected for study — 22.

APPENDIX V

A Model of Forestry-based Integrated Rural Development Programme

(An innovation for alleviation of rural poverty)

Here is a model comprising of chain of interlinked schemes, to be implemented by Forest Department or Social Forestry Department on available forest area (or on village panchayat land in concurrence with local G.P.) near a village, aimed at achieving improvement in quality of village life.

The following write-up shall illustrate the model. The scheme shall be implemented during a period of 5 years in the first phase.

Since this is an innovation which still needs testing — before taking up a massive programmes of the type, it shall be advisable to first operate the project on a pilot basis with a view to know its practicability and teething troubles, if any.

To start with 40 ha area (with scope for irrigation) shall be selected near a village with a population of 1000, or say 200 families.

(A) Individual Beneficiary Scheme

Twenty-five poorest of the poor families of that village shall be selected, preferably from amongst adivasis and other backward castes, who are willing to work on the project.

(i) *Rehabilitation of poor, homeless people* — Twenty-five semi-permanent hutments shall be constructed on a suitable site in the area to accommodate these families.

(ii) *Supply of milch cattle* — (Diary Development) — Each family shall be provided with 2 high yielding milch cattle under I.R.D.P. or through Bank, if necessary (The Forest Department shall give surety for advance of loan for purchase of cattle). The department shall also make arrangement for artificial insemination of ordinary cows after bringing them at one place.

(iii) *Creation of Gothas near Villages* — A permanent cattle shed with a capacity to accommodate 50 cattle shall be constructed with arrangements to stall feed the cattle.

(iv) *Installation of Bio-gas plants* – The entire dung shall be fed to a community bio-gas plant of capacity 35 m^3 which shall be installed near cattle shed and hutments. The cow-dung produced from 50 cattle will in turn generate 1000 ft^3 gas, daily.

(v) *Construction of latrines* – Two sanitary blocks consisting of 5 units each (Separately for ladies and gents) shall be constructed with their outlets connected to the Gas plant. This will produce additional 125 ft^3 bio-gas.

Popularisation of Non-conventional Energy Sources

With these arrangements, the gas produced by anaerobic fermentation of all organic matter inside the bio-gas plant shall be sufficient to meet the domestic needs of the 25 families.

The dung slurry coming out of the plant (about 250 MT in a year), shall be used as organic manure in pasture development, permanent nursery, gardening and various plantation activities undertaken inside the area. About 50 MT. slurry may be sufficient to meet the requirements of various activities inside the area. Surplus slurry (about 200 MT.) may either be used in other departmental nurseries or sold at market prices.

Intensive Development of Fodder Resources

A suitable area of 5 ha shall be earmarked for fodder development, para green grass and berseem shall be cultivated in patches of 1/2 ha each while in the remaining 4 ha area, grasses and legumes such as *Stylo*, *Mushi, Marvel, Gujraj* etc. shall be introduced. *Hamata* shall also be grown in the available space between rows of plantsin the energy plantation. All these shall be grown under irrigated conditions and harvested — periodically.

The grasses mixed with suitable proportion of Subabul leaves and cattle feed shall be sufficient to feed the cattle round the year. Surplus fodder shall be sold to local — Gram Panchayat on cutting basis.

The supply of grass to the 25 families shall be free of cost. However cutting of grass and feeding the cattle shall have to be done by them.

Nursery Under E.G.S.

A permanent nursery shall be created under E.G.S. in an area of 2 ha with a view to providing work round the year to at least one adult member of each family.

The choice of species and number of plants to be raised in the Nursery shall be guided by the following considerations

(i) Requirement of irrigated energy plantation inside the project area.
(ii) Requirement of ornamental and fruit plants to be planted in Forest Park, along avenues, inspection paths and on all available vacant patches inside the area.
(iii) Requirement of local villages for planting in their fields, kitchen gardens, waste lands, compounds of educational and other institutions etc.
(iv) Requirement of nearby afforestation schemes.

Few grafted plants shall also be included in the planting stock.

On an average 4 lakh poly bag plants may be raised every year.

Irrigated Energy Plantation Under E.G.S.

A high density energy plantation under irrigated — conditions shall be raised in an area of 25 ha, to be selected at one place or in patches where soil depth is atleast 30 cm.

The following fast growing species with high calorific value may be considered for planting in 5 ha area each at spacings of 1m X 1m, 1m X 2m, 1m X 3m, 1.5m X 1.5m, 2m X 2m in each hectare.

Subabul, Suru, Prosopis, Neam, Ramkethi babul
Total No. of plants (5 X 25277) : 1.26, 385.

The above species shall be grown and harvested under similar conditions to facilities comparative study of biomass production. Subsequently, choice of species, spacing, incidence of irrigation, and rotation shall be modified based on the — experience gained from the above studies.

This work will generate additional labour potential of 45000 mandays to provide work to other labourers from the village.

Pre-monsoon planting shall be carried out and the plantation shall be maintained for 4.5 years, taking full advantage of 5 growing seasons.

Opening of Fuelwood Depots

The plantation shall be exploited after 4.5 years and the entire felled material shall be collected in a fuelwood adopt to be established in the same area. Fuel wood and poles shall be supplied to local villagers at concessional rates. The area can be replanted after 5 years or advantage of coppice growth may be taken. Alternatively, 5 ha area may be exploited and replanted every year. The material obtained shall be sufficient to meet the requirements of fuelwood and small wood of the local villagers.

Supply of Bullock-carts to Adivasis

Entire transport in the area shall be done by bullock carts 5 bullock-carts shall be enough for the purpose. These will provide additional income to the owners, without any expenditure on maintenance.

Supply of Fruit Plants to Adivasis

One Coconut plant (*Hawiin* var), one lemon plant, one Papaya plant, one Peru plant and one Mango plant (all grafted) shall be supplied to each family, to be planted in their respective kitchen gardens. They shall also be encouraged to grow seasonal vegetables in their respective gardens. The boundaries of garden may be demarcated by one metre wide fencing of close spaced Subabul plants. This shall project the vegetable against hot winds, provide leaf fodder for cattle and improve nutrient status of sub-soil. The beneficiaries shall be permitted to use dung slurry as fertilizer free of cost for growing vegetables.

Surplus vegetables may be sold by the growers on market days to earn extra income.

Creation of Forest Park

A forest park shall be developed in an area on one ha by planting ornamental trees, creating lawns, a rosary with proper layout and providing cement benches so that this makes a picnic spot for catering to recreational and aesthetic needs of the villagers.

Honey Collection

Five Bee boxes with bees shall be kept at suitable places inside the area and honey shall be extracted periodically.

Poultry Farming

Each family shall be supplied with 5 white leg horn chics in the first year. The eggs obtained (200 per chic per year) shall be collected by the beneficiaries and marketed as per arrangements made by the Department or Cooperative Society of the beneficiaries.

Managerial Mechanism of the Project

One R.F.O. shall be made responsible for execution of all activities under the project. He shall be stationed preferably inside or as near the project area as possible. He shall be required to maintain liaison with concerned departments and agencies and shall work under the guidance and control of the Divisional Forest Officer and Assistant Conservator of Forests. The routine activities of plantation, nursery etc. shall be carried out by the local guards and foresters.

In a nutshell, land utilisation pattern will be as below:

Irrigation plantation	..25 ha
Nursery	.. 2 ha
Pasture Development	.. 5 ha
Forest Park	.. 1 ha
Labour colony, Bio-gas plant, cattleshed, kondwara, kitchen, gardens etc.	.. 5 ha
Area to be kept vacant for any unforeseen use.	.. 2 ha
Total	..40 ha

Salient Features of the Scheme

1. Twenty-five poorest of the poor families are lifted above poverty line. Moreover, they become permanently immune to hazards of any scarcity situation that may arise in future.
2. Optimum and fullest utilisation of available human, material and natural resources (such as land and water) is achieved.
3. The schemes are integrated in a manner that the wastes are either recycled or minimised.
4. Though conventional nursery and plantation schemes are not revenue oriented, but this scheme fit the norms of benefit cost analysis even during the first phase. An after infrastructure is created by initial capital investment, this shall be a self generating project, giving substantial return perpetually.
5. This shall create tremendous demonstrative impact and induce other farmers having irrigated lands to take up similar projects. Thus Social forestry programmes will get a boost.
6. Reduced biotic interferences shall be of considerable help in preservation of forest wealth, or whatever is left of it. At the same time, better success shall be achieved in plantation schemes.
7. Increased production of milk, and creation of green belts all around shall be stride in while Revolution and Green Revolution.
8. The project shall provide scope for development of cottage industries based on forest produce (for example, basket making, rope making, tusser cultivation etc.) on a Co-operative basis giving fillip to cooperative movement. Agave and bamboo may be exploited periodically and raw material used for basket making, rope making etc. by Cooperative Societies of the beneficiaries.
9. This shall be an ideal solution to the problem of rehabilitation/ resettlement of project affected or displaced persons.

And all this shall be over and above innumerable intangible social benefits of tree plantation.

Who gains/achieves what from the project

A. *Poor Adivasis (Forest Labourers)*

(i) Free houses in clean, natural environment
(ii) Free supply of gas for domestic consumption
(iii) Work at door step round the year.
(iv) Average income per family @ Rs. 45 daily

B. *Village*

(i) Increased production of milk, vegetables, eggs, honey, fuel, fruits, fodder, fertilizers etc.
(ii) Labour intensive scheme to provide employment to — villagers.
(iii) All round greenery and hence better environment.

C. *Forest Department*

(i) Implementation of various schemes at one place with assured success and at minimum cost.
(ii) Substantial returns on investment.
(iii) Assistance to other departments in implementation of their schemes or achievements of targets.
(iv) Goodwill and cooperation of people, other departments and political leadership.
(v) A permanent solution to the problems of illicit fellings (other than organised) and encroachments, since the — persons normally indulging in these activities are weaned away.

D. *Nation*

(i) Implementation of national priority programmes such as 20 point programmes, family planning programmes, small saving programmes etc. etc.
(ii) Increased area under tree cover.
(iii) Increase in G.N.P.
(iv) Reversal of trend in urbanisation and above all.
(v) Improvement in quality of village life.

The implementation of this kind of project has already been started in village *Erandgaon on Yeola Vinchur road* at a distance of about 80 km from *Nashik*.

An area of 10 ha (GP land) adjoining an existing well was — selected and schemes of nursery and plantation get sanctioned under NREP.

Five Adiwasi families of Erandgaon living below poverty line cards were selected and provided with five hutments constructed in the same area. A 7 m^3 capacity bio-gas plant has been installed and is functioning satisfactorily. Each family has been given one buffalo under IRDP. The beneficiaries have sown *hameta, cenchrus, Jawari* etc. in 1 ha patch. This helps in meeting the fodder requirement of cattle partly. Plantation of fuel wood species in 5 ha was done in August, 84 Nursery of 2 lakhs plants is in progress.

Remaining schemes are at various stages of introduction (Model proposed by V.K. Mohan D.F.O., East Nashik.)

BIBLIOGRAPHY

Deogaonkar (Dr.), S.G. *The Madia of Bhamragad,* Concept Publishing Company, New Delhi, 1982.

Deogaonkar (Dr.), S.G. *Problems of Development of Tribal Areas,* Leeladevi Publications, New Delhi, 1980.

Deogaonkar (Dr.) S.G. *Tribal Exploitation,* Inter-India Pub., New Delhi, 1990.

Mehta (Dr.), B.H. *Gonds of Central Indian Highlands,* Concept Publishing Company, New Delhi, 1984.

Maharashtra State. *Report on the Evaluation of the Scheme of Rehabilitation of Shifting Cultivators in Chanda District,* Tribal Research Institute, Poona, 1969.

Maharashtra State. *Sub-Plan for Adivasis Maharashtra State—A Summary (1974-1979),* Social Welfare Cultural Department, Bombay — 1974.

Maharashtra State. *Project Report on Primitive Tribes Madia — Gonds in Bhamragad Area of Chandrapur District — Proposed plan for 1980-81 to 1984-85* — VI Plan Period.

Government of Maharashtra. *Evaluation Study of Integrated Development Project — Gadchiroli-I — Etapalli, Tribal Research & Training Institute,* Pune, November 1985.

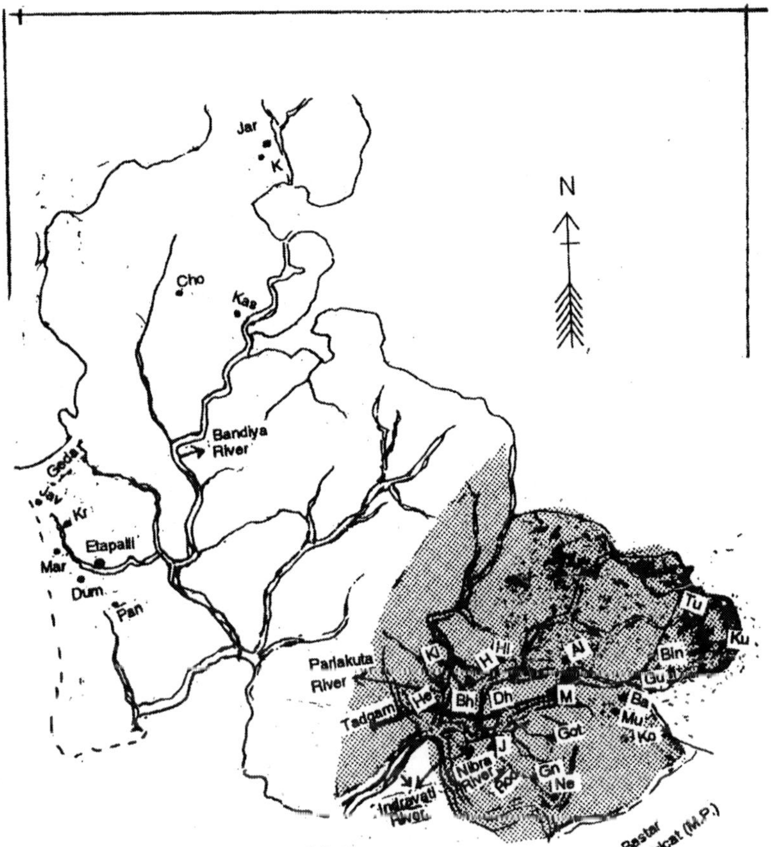

Maharashtra State

ETAPALLI [dist. Gadchiroli]

Panchayat Samiti Area

(I.T.D.P. Etapalli and I.T.D.P. (Primitive Tribe) Bhamragad Villages from I.T.D.P.

Etapalli

Etapalli Geda

Jar	Jarawandi
K	Kandhli
Kas	Kasansur
Cho	Chokhewada
Kr	Krishnar
Jav	Javelli
Dum	Dumme
Pan	Pandhewahi

(Total: Ten)

Villages from I.T.D.P. (Primitive Tribes)

Hills

Bhamragad

Al	Aldandi (Haldandi)	Ne	Nelgunda
Bh	Bhamragad	Bod	Bodange
Dh	Dhodraj	Gn	Gongwada
Tu	Turremarka	M	Malampoddur
Bin	Binagunda	He	Hemalkosa
Ku	Kuvvakodi	J	Juvvi
Gu	Gundenhod	Hi	Hiddur
Ba	Bangadi	H	Hitapadi
Mu	Murangal	Ki	Kiyar
Ko	Koyar	A	Arewada
Got	Gotpadi	L	Laheri

(Total: Twenty-two)

INDEX

Aayakut scheme, 58
Accessibility, 13, 19
Acculturation, 106
Action plan, 161
Additional chief secretary, 154
Additional coverage, 44
Additional tribal commissioner, 43
Adivasis, 193
Adivasi Cooperative Society (ACS), 40, 57, 99, 146, 148
Administrative organisation, 148
Adult education programmes, 59, 95
Aeroplane, 89, 127
Agricultural economy, 13
    inputs, 67, 124
Aheri, 15, 63
    implemented schemes, 63-64
    tribal development officer, 121, 123
    zamindari, 17, 25
Aldandi, 83, 171
Allapalli schemes, 64
Ambil, 28, 30
Amravati, 44, 56
Anganwadi, 84, 93, 108, 109, 128, 133, 147
    schemes, 134
    workers, 132
Animal husbandry, 59, 66, 85, 89, 91, 92, 101, 139, 143
    training, 105, 136
        centre, 64
Anti-public, 167
Applied nutrition programmes, 59
Arewada, 21, 84, 171
Ashram schools, 47, 57, 108, 130
    complex, 40, 146
Attributes, 141
Attitudinal changes, 142
Auxiliary Nurse-cum Midwives (ANM), 131, 135

Baba Amte, 127
Bada-Madia, 26, 68
    village, 87
Bakshis, 106, 107
Balwadis, 58, 128
    students, 132
Bamboo collection, 113
    walls, 156
Bandiya rivers, 25, 29
Bangadi, 83
Below poverty level, 98
Beneficiaries, 15, 16, 18, 21, 71, 82, 86, 92, 105, 108, 112, 115, 119, 136, 144, 146
    list of, 171-72
    schemes, 14, 125, 135
Benthmite formula, 160
Benefits-scheme-wise, evaluation of, 119
Bhagats, 97
Bhamragad, 15, 18, 60, 66, 70, 71, 73, 74, 76, 78, 80, 83, 86, 87, 91, 101, 105, 125, 133, 171
    blocks, 17
    primitive tribes area, 20, 186
    revenue circle, 187
    schemes implemented, 22
Bhartiya Adimjati Sevak Sangh (BAJSS), 117
Binagunda, 83, 88, 90, 173
Black-magic, 97
Bodange, 91, 173
Bodis (small lake), 102
    construction of, 138
Brahmapuri, 24
Brick-making, 84, 120

Bride-price, 157
British regime, 156
Budget, 37
Bulldozers, 67, 90, 143
Bullock-carts, 84, 85, 95, 102, 108, 138, 144
  schemes, 119

Central Government, 40, 150
Chairman Panchayat Samiti, 27
Challenges, 152
Chandrapur district, 24, 39, 44
Child marriage, 157
Chillies, 93
Chokhewada, 111, 181
Chota-madia, 26, 88
  shifting cultivators, 103
Communication facilities, 158
Community development programme, 51
Constraints, 15, 16
Cooperative societies, 56
Credit facilities, 60, 148

Dairy department, 59
Dancing equipment, 129
Decentralisation, 158
Demonstration, 88, 96, 126, 144
Dhakkan, 90
Dhodraj village, 91, 103, 173
Dhurve Gond, 25
Diesel, sources of, 86
Divorce, 157
Drinking water, 30, 83, 91, 147
  facilities, 106, 107

Education, 66, 158
Educational research training organisation, 129
Eighth Five Year Plan, 161, 167, 168
Electric pump, 121, 122
Electrification, 139
Elwin, Verrier, 148, 161
Employment Guarantee Schemes, 60
  programmes, 169
Equality, 13
Etapalli, 15, 17, 66, 182
  panchayat samiti, 17, 24, 95, 113
  schemes implemented, 23
  Zilla Parishad school, 114
Evaluation, 133
Exploitation, 13, 141, 160
Excise policy, 38

Fair-price shop, 93
Family welfare programmes, 59
  planning, 176
Fertilisers, 124
Festivals, 28
Field investigation, 19
Fish-seed, 86
Fishermen's Cooperative Society, 86, 125
Fodder resources, intensive development of, 191
Food drink, 29
Food and eating habits, 28
Forest labour cooperative societies, 60
Forestry-based integrated development model, 145
  programme, 190
Fraternity, 13
Fruits, 29

Gadchiroli district, 15, 24, 25, 44, 121, 146
  action plan, 162
  implemented schemes, 64, 68, 70, 71
Gaita (patel), 19
Gayatas (patels), 20, 90, 110
Geda, 114
German, 30
Ghotuls, 19, 20, 26, 70, 87, 89, 91, 98, 105, 111, 126
Goat-keeping (poultry), 125
Gobar-gas/Biogas, 67
Gobar-gas plants, 111, 112, 117, 121, 159
  scheme, 116
Gonds, 25
Gondwada, 93, 174
Gotpadi, 94, 175
Government hostels, 57
Government of India, 39, 151
Gram (*Chana*), 132
Gram Panchayats, 146
Grant-in-aid ashram schools, 57

Ground-nut, 89
Growth centres, 40, 146
Gundenhod, 93, 175

Haimendorf, Christoph Von-Fourer,
 161
Haryana, 136, 139
Hemalkasa, 97, 99, 125, 175
Hiddur, 100, 176
Hitapadi, 100, 176
Honey collection, 29, 194
Horticulture, 58, 126, 163
 plantation farm, 117

Individual beneficiary schemes, 119, 190
Indravati rivers, 25, 29
Industrialisation, 141
Integrated Area Development
 Approach, 37
Integrated child development schemes,
 14, 131
 envisaged objectives of, 131
Integrated Tribal Development
 Programmes, 13, 18, 22, 77, 78, 80,
 111, 148, 181
 schemes implemented in, 60
 special central assistance, 62
 villages, 185
Irrigated energy plantation, 192
Irrigation facilities, 103
 schemes, 161

Jaggery (*Gur*), 132
Jalgaon, 44
Janata model type, 112
Jarawandi, 115, 182
Javelli, 116, 183
Juvvi, 101, 177

Kandholi, 116, 183
Kasansur, 116, 184
Katkaris, 14, 82
Khatulwar Gond, 25
Kitchen garden, 89
Kiyar, 177
Kolaba district, 39
Koyar, 177
Krishnar, 117, 184

Kuccha forest, 25, 128
Kusari, 106
 cultivation, 111
Kuvvakodi, 83, 104, 107, 178

Land development banks, 60
Leheri, 91, 78
Lok-Biradari prakalpa, 97, 103, 125
Loans, 115
Lugda (nine yard sarees), 27

Machinery for implementation, 41-42
Madia dancers, 129
Madia-farmer's land, improvement of,
 138
Madia-Gonds, 14, 17, 24, 25, 26, 39, 82
Madia's marriages, 137
Madia-shibir, 127
Madia-women, 27, 28
Maharashtra, 14, 24, 37, 73, 74
 population, 45
Maharashtra State Cooperative Tribal
 Development, 57, 63
Maharashtra, tribal sub-plan in, 43-45
Maharogi Seva Samiti, 125
Mahua wine, 29
Malpractices, 135
Malampoddar, 108, 179
Mangalore, 103, 128
Marriages, 28, 137, 157
Masahat, 18
Mechanical inputs, 139
Meta (means hill), 88
Metal-work training, 102
Methodology, 17, 18
Minimum needs programmes, 131
Minor forest produce, purchase of, 57
Mitra, Sunil, 164
Modified area development approach,
 44
Monopoly grain purchase scheme, 57
Murangal, 109, 180
Myrobalans, collection of, 29

Nagpur University, 118
Nanded, 44
Nasik, 43, 56
National Development Council, 167

Nationalised Banks, 60
Navrang mandal, 118
Naxalite activity, 161
Nehru, Jawaharlal, 148
Nelgunda, 110, 180
New trend, 148
Non-conventional energy sources, 191
Non-divertability, 37
Non-lapsability, 38
Non-vegetarians, 28, 156
Nucleus budget, 14, 60, 68, 70, 112
    allotment, 74
    expenditure, 71, 72, 73, 74, 81
    schemes, 65
Nullas, 88, 111
Nutrition programmes, 163

Oil-engine, 102, 117, 120
Oil-engine pumps, information, 121
Onions, 89, 93
Operating officers, 21
Opinions, 141
Organisational set-up, 153
Outside tribal sub-plan area, 46

Palakmantri, 43
Pamal-Gautam rivers, 25
Panchayati Raj system, 169
Panchayat samiti, 15, 17, 57, 64, 66, 67, 111, 124
Pandhevahi, 184
Parlakota rivers, 25
Pattas, 105
Pattis, 17
Peka poriya madkami, 84
Penda, 30, 90, 100, 104, 106
People's forest policy stressed, 164
Persapen (*Bada deo*), 167, 168
Polyandry, 157
Polygynny, 157
Population, 111, 132
Post-basic ashram schools, 47, 57
Poultry, 89, 125
    farming, 117, 127, 194
Poverty, 157
Pradhans, 25
Prakashtha upakarans, 64, 136
Primary Health Centres (PHC), 66, 87, 113, 162
Primitive tribes, 76, 78
    project, 17, 18
Prohibition, 39, 141
Project advisory committee, 154
Public health department, 59
Public works department schemes, 65
Pujas (Pandums), 28
Punjabrao Krishi Vidyapeeth, 138

Railway train, 89, 127
Raj-Gonds, 25
Rasta-Roko, 106
Recruitment policy, 151
Remarriage, 157
Road communication, 107, 157
    facilities, 67
Roofing of huts, 119, 138
Rural electrification, 161
Rural development schemes, 59
Rural poverty, alleviation of, 190

Sahukars, 107
Samaj Mandir (community centre), 91, 96, 110, 126
Sarpanch, 85, 107
Scheduled tribe families, 52
    population, 45
Schemes, implementation of, 38, 43, 82
    salient features of, 195
School complex scheme, 59
Secretariat (mantralaya) level, 56
Self-employment schemes, 60
Seventh Five Year Plan, 44
Shifting cultivation, 30, 90, 100, 104, 106
Silver-belt (*Kamarpatta*), 28
Sironcha, 15, 24
Special Central Assistance (SCA), 14, 76, 77, 79, 80, 103
Special executive committee, 43
Soil conservation scheme, 58
Solar-tube lights, 129
Social welfare department, 59
State education department, 58
Steering committee, 41
Sukli, 132

Tadgaon, 86

Teacher's training, 59
Tendu leaves, 29
Tenets, 37
Tobacco, 29, 89
Tractor, 92
    ploughing, 95, 159
Tribal Area Research Unit, 113
Tribal beneficiaries, 16, 98
Tribal commissioner, 42
    culture, 156
    development, perspective for, 161
        programmes, 56
Tribal Research and Training Institute (TRTI), 17
Tribal students, book-banks schemes, 58
Tribal sub-plan, 14, 37, 46
    administrative set-up, 42
    schemes, 14, 146
    strategy, 82
Turremarka, 111, 180
TV set, 113
20-point programme, 124

Unified command approach, 37
Uniforms, distribution of, 128
Unmarried girls, 27

Vatte Sonya Atram, 108
Vegetables, 126
Village councils, 169
    community, 147
Village-wise evaluation, 82
Voluntary organisations, 59, 118

Warora, 24, 125
Widow-dressing, 90
Woollen-blankets, 135

Yeotmal, 44, 56

Zamindari, 17, 25
Zharoo Kharidi, 92
Zilla Parishad, 57, 59, 66, 94, 113, 129
    school, 20, 113, 114
Zoo, 127